C0-ATN-434

THE TIMES *management library*

tml

The Cost of Quality

The Cost of Quality

J. M. Groocock

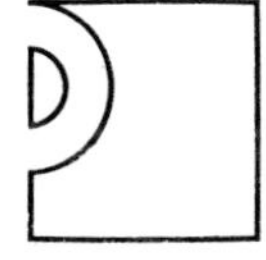

Pitman Publishing

First published 1974

Sir Isaac Pitman and Sons Ltd.
Pitman House, Parker Street, Kingsway, London, WC2B 5PB
P.O. Box 46038, Banda Street, Nairobi, Kenya

Sir Isaac Pitman (Aust.) Pty. Ltd.
Pitman House, 158 Bouverie Street, Carlton, Victoria 3053, Australia

Pitman Publishing Corporation
6 East 43rd Street, New York, N.Y. 10017, U.S.A.

Sir Isaac Pitman (Canada) Ltd.
495 Wellington Street West, Toronto 135, Canada

The Copp Clark Publishing Company
517 Wellington Street West, Toronto 135, Canada

ISBN: 0 273 31695 8

Text set in 10/11 pt Monotype Times Roman, printed by letterpress, and bound in Great Britain at The Pitman Press, Bath

G4—(TML 17:51)

To Sheila

Preface

Books on quality control have been written by many different types of authors—by professional statisticians, by consultants, by teachers in technical colleges and universities and by industrial engineers and general managers having a special interest in quality. Each of these groups has had its own contribution to make to the development of the subject. This book is written by a full-time quality manager, who for the past twelve years has managed quality departments within a large international company—International Telephone and Telegraph Corporation—first as quality manager of a division making transistors, diodes, and other semiconductor devices, then as company quality manager of a major subsidiary—Standard Telephones and Cables—one of the UK's largest manufacturers of telecommunications equipment, and for the last four years as Director–Quality of ITT Europe, a group of companies of nearly 200,000 employees making a very wide range of products in 180 manufacturing plants throughout western Europe. With this background the approach to the book is necessarily personal. The book does not attempt to summarize previously published work—this is best done by writers with an academic background—but depends upon the writer's own experience of the development and application of quality systems within the framework of a single, broad-based company.

This book is written not only to help quality managers achieve their objectives, but also to give general managers and managers of departments other than Quality an understanding of the overall quality system of their companies and the part they themselves must play if quality objectives are to be achieved.

In the early 1960s quality control was of particular importance in the semiconductor industry. Mass-produced semiconductor devices were ideal for statistical quality control and the complex technology demanded refined process control. The pressures to procure military electronic equipment required the development of sophisticated specifications and quality-assurance procedures. At that time transistors were the key component dominating the reliability of electronic equipment and a thorough knowledge of reliability was therefore essential for quality managers in the industry. For the writer this need was enhanced by work on the development of accelerated life-test methods undertaken on contracts from the UK Government and later in developing the quality and reliability-assurance procedures applied to the first high-reliability transistors used in the repeaters of transoceanic-communication cables. This experience served as a background for the technical aspects of the book.

Until P. B. Crosby became Director–Quality of ITT in 1965, this vast international corporation had no overall quality policy or standard practices, although, of course, many of its constituent units were in the forefront of the application of quality control. During the past eight years, a series of advanced quality systems has been developed and applied to ITT as a whole, first in its telecommunications and electronic operations and then, as the corporation itself developed, in a progressively wider range of industries—consumer and industrial products, the food industry, hotels, insurance and so on.

Initially the quality-council system was established and Crosby's original work on zero defects was expanded into an integrated quality-improvement programme. The ITT quality-cost reporting system was developed first in Europe and then applied throughout all of the corporation's operations. Later quality-cost control was integrated into ITT's general business-planning system. Quality-status reporting was developed both in Europe and North and Latin America and in the Far East. More recently the corporation has established an organizational framework to implement the policy of assuring that all new products are qualification tested before sale to customers. Again, much of this system was developed in Europe before being applied throughout the corporation. Another advance has been the application of a systematic quality-auditing procedure. Surmounting all these technical advances has been Crosby's insistence upon the importance of management interest and participation in quality activities and his success in achieving this.

The writer's views on quality have been shaped during his years with ITT and he gives grateful acknowledgement to his ITT colleagues in both Quality and other departments. Principal among these is P. B. Crosby himself and also from the USA E. W. Karlin. Of the writer's many European colleagues he would specifically mention G. Borel of France and H. Blanco Lozellier of Spain, respectively President and Vice-President of the European Organization for Quality Control in 1972, J. Stievenart of Belgium and A. C. Brown of the UK. Finally, the general management of ITT as a whole, including the President of ITT Europe, M. C. Bergerac, has provided a framework of support, participation and demand in which the quality function could do its whole job.

The writer also expresses his gratitude to his secretary, Mrs A. Luloff, who typed the book.

Extracts from BS 9001: 1967 *Sampling procedures and tables for inspection by attributes for electronic parts of assessed quality* and BS 9301 N002: 1971 *Detail specification for general purpose signal diode . . . 150 mA, 150 V* are reproduced by permission of the British Standards Institution, 2 Park Street, London W1A 2BS.

6 February 1973

Contents

		page
	Preface	vii
1	**Quality in the Business**	1
	Quality, product definition, conformance—Policies for quality	
2	**Quality Cost Reporting**	8
	Quality, price and value—Definition and categorization of quality costs—Prevention, appraisal and failure quality costs—Comptroller responsibilities for quality-cost measuring—The purposes of quality-cost reporting—Quality-cost indices—Wider aspects of quality costs	
3	**Quality Management**	30
	Quality problem solving—Organization of the quality department—The relationship of inspection, test, quality and manufacturing—The organizational position of the quality department—Staff quality directors, quality managers and quality councils	
4	**The Quality-Improvement Programme**	46
	Management commitment—The quality-improvement team—Quality measurement and quality-cost reporting—Quality awareness—Corrective action—Defect-prevention audit—Zero defects—Goal-setting, error-cause removal and recognition	

5 **The Quality Department and the General Manager** 73

Quality reports—Targets for quality-cost reduction and quality-manpower control—Consolidated quality reports—Quality department recruiting and training

6 **Inspection by Sampling** 84

One hundred per cent inspection—Inspection by sampling—Theory of attribute sampling—Producer's risk and consumer's risk—AQL and LTPD—BS 9001 and MIL-STD-19500—Testing by the producer or the consumer—Inspection levels and lot sizes—Isolated lot and series of lots—Setting the AQL—Setting the inspection level—Acceptance inspection, quality auditing and management action

7 **Supplier Quality Control** 115

Purchasing specifications—Supplier approval—Qualification approval—Continuing quality assurance—Electronic parts of assessed quality

8 **Quality Control of New Products** 130

Quality engineers in development—Design review—Qualification testing—Organization for qualification testing—Error control in engineering

9 **Quality and Reliability** 148

The reliability problem—Making reliable products—Redundancy—Accelerated life testing—Physics of failure—System effectiveness—Management for reliability

10 **Case Studies** 161

Start of a zero defects programme—Qualification test of the AB 357

Annotated Reading List 174

Index 176

1 Quality in the Business

Quality control has been used by management for many decades and all contemporary managers within manufacturing industry have some acquaintanceship with it. However, there is no agreement amongst them on the objectives of quality control and the place of quality control within the business structure. To many managers quality control is a set of techniques, based upon mathematical statistics, and applied by small groups of specialists, mainly in technologically advanced industries. To others it is simply a new name for inspection and test: to others it is something that powerful customers, particularly government agencies, insist upon, and which has a major customer-relations content. Yet others believe the quality-control department has sole responsibility for the quality of the product and others again that quality control is mainly concerned with workmanship.

The concept of quality itself is a difficult one, open to many individual interpretations both in common usage and within professional quality control. Phrases that are frequently used are: "a top-quality product", "the quality is poor", "we have got a quality problem", "if you want good quality you must pay for it" and "quality, price and delivery". Formal definitions of quality have been given by many writers and also by quality-control organizations. (For example, definitions of quality, quality of design and quality of conformance are included in the *Glossary of Terms Used in Quality Control*, published by the European Organization for Quality Control in 1969). Recently, P. B. Crosby has given emphasis to the conformance aspects of quality and has said simply: "Quality means conformance." In practice, this turns out to be the definition of quality most useful to workers in quality control. It converts quality from a concept of almost mystical complexity into a quantitatively measurable tool. It is the definition of quality which will be used in this book.

A business then has two quality objectives. These are:

(i) to supply products to customers that conform to their requirements;
(ii) to minimize quality costs.

It might be thought that these two objectives are incompatible and that quality control would be concerned with achieving the best balance between the two. In practice this is not so. The concepts of defect prevention and of doing any task correctly the first time enable both objectives to be achieved simultaneously. This is one of the most important principles of modern quality control.

The meaning of product conformance will be discussed in detail later in this chapter, and Chapter 2 will be devoted entirely to quality costs. A description of the means of achieving the two objectives of the quality system will be the major aim of the book as a whole.

In the past, formal quality control has been applied almost exclusively to manufactured products—to "hardware" of all kinds—and this book will deal mainly with this aspect of quality control. However, it is noteworthy that the principles of quality control are applicable beyond product manufacture. In all human activities error is possible and, in the absence of planned error prevention, almost inevitable The consequence of error is either that the result of the activity is inferior to the aim or that more effort must be spent in detecting the effects of the error and correcting them. Professional quality control is now starting to be applied in a number of service industries: in insurance, in car hire, in the hotel industry, and it is possible that service industry will see the major extension of the application of quality control in the future.

QUALITY, PRODUCT DEFINITION AND CONFORMANCE[1]

When a sale is made, the vendor promises to supply a particular product by a certain date for a certain price. For the price and delivery, there is usually no problem of communication: the vendor and the customer know without effort what has been promised. The product description is more difficult. The vendor may simply promise to supply a product that will "wash all your clothes", or he may hand over a

[1] This section is based on an article by the author published in *Electronics and Power*, December 1970.

1,000-page specification. In either case, however, the vendor should know exactly what he is intending to supply. If he does, he can make a professional judgement about whether the customer will be pleased with it. If he does not, whether or not the customer is pleased is a matter of luck.

The next stage in pleasing the customer is to conform to the promised delivery, to conform to the quoted price and to conform to the product description given to the customer. However, beyond this, the product should be exactly as the vendor intended it to be.

Conformance to What?

The price and delivery are easily described, but the product is not. In fact, the product is described in a series of specifications that should be defined during the marketing and design phases of the introduction of a new product.

There are three different types of manufacturing specifications having the following functions:

(i) to describe how the product should be made;
(ii) to describe what the product should be;
(iii) to describe what the product should do.

The first type of specification includes process specifications, tooling specifications, component specifications, etc. The second includes drawings, models of the product, workmanship standards, etc. The third includes the performance specifications, reliability specifications, and so on. These specifications have purposes concerned with manufacturing efficiency, in addition to their product-definition purposes.

It is implicit in the above analysis that attention is concentrated upon a particular product, and that the three types of manufacturing specifications apply to that product. For example, if the product is a particular television set the specifications describing how the set should be made will include the specifications to which the cathode-ray tube, the transistors, capacitors, resistors and other components from which the set is assembled, are purchased. However, the television-set specifications will not usually define how these components are to be made; they will only define what they are required to do and, to some extent, what they must be. On the other hand, if the product upon which attention is concentrated is, say, a particular capacitor, the manufacturing specifications for the capacitor *will* define how it is to be made.

In principle, a complete description of how the product should be made will define it exactly, and it should not then be necessary to specify the product or its performance. Similarly, if the product is described exactly, it should not be necessary to specify its performance, because this will already be fixed. (The converse is not true: there may be many ways of making the same product, and different products may have the same performance.)

In addition to the three types of manufacturing specifications describing the product, there are three corresponding types of quality-control specifications, defining the methods to be used in checking how well the product conforms to the manufacturing specifications. These are:

(i) how the product should be made: process audits, incoming inspection specifications, machine check procedures, etc.

(ii) what the product should be: in-process and final inspection specifications, etc.

(iii) what the product should do: qualification, in-process and final test specifications, reliability-test specifications, environmental-test specifications, field-trial programmes, etc.

This matrix of specifications is summarized in Table 1.1.

TABLE 1.1

Product Description

Purpose	Manufacturing specifications	Quality-control specifications	Actuality	What the customer is told
how should it be made?	piecepart and process specifications, etc.	incoming inspection specifications, process audits, etc.	how was it made?	claimed process
what should it be?	drawings, models, etc.	in-process and final inspection specifications, etc.	what is it?	advertised description
what should it do?	performance, reliability, specifications, etc.	in-process and final-test specifications, reliability-test specifications, etc.	what does it do?	claimed performance

Each existing product will have been made in a particular way, it will actually be a particular item and it will have an actual performance. The quality-control specifications enable the correspondence between the actuality and the manufacturing specifications to be evaluated.

It is clear that complete specifications of how to make a product, what it should be and what it should do, together with the three corresponding types of quality-control specifications, introduce considerable redundancy. This is fortunate, because it is usually impracticable to complete all the six types of specifications, and, for different products, principal reliance, for quality control, is placed on one or the other type. For a simple chemical or a simple mechanical component, the product itself can be specified. Thus, 99·97 per cent ethyl alcohol defines the compound precisely; how it is made is not very important, and it is unnecessary to specify its properties because these are completely fixed and widely known.

For a pharmaceutical or an electronic component, the main emphasis may be on the performance specifications, e.g. the biological activity of an antibiotic or the electrical characteristics of a transistor. However, for products of this type, the emphasis sometimes has to be put on the test specification rather than on the performance specification. Instead of specifying that the transistor shall have a minimum gain of 20, it is specified that, when tested in a particular circuit with a base current of 1 mA at a frequency of 100 MHz, the collector current shall be a minimum of 20 mA.

For some characteristics of some products, the test specification does not give a satisfactory means of ensuring conformance to the performance specification. One can specify the required performance, e.g. that the transistor shall have a twenty-year life and a failure rate always below 10^{-9} per hour, or that the pharmaceutical compound can be taken regularly for twenty years without producing cancer in more than one person in 100,000; but there is no satisfactory way of testing for such performance. In these cases, often the best that can be done is to place reliance on the precise specification and conformance control of the manufacturing method.

For any product, a conscious decision should be made about the key specification types for defining the product and ensuring conformance. For some products, the method of manufacture can be varied at the convenience of the manufacturing department, because conformance is determined by the performance specification. For others, process control is vital. For some products, test methods can be changed without concern; for others they are crucial.

In the previous sections, the assumption has been made that responsibility for adequate product description and conformance control rests with the vendor. Sometimes the customer may take over at least part of this responsibility by specifying in detail the product that he wishes to buy or the performance it should achieve. The customer may even define the quality-control specifications that must be used to check conformance.

Under these circumstances, there is justification for the vendor limiting his responsibility to supplying a product that conforms to the customer's specifications. But this only happens with the most sophisticated organizational customers. Usually, it is also necessary for the vendor to make a judgement about the customer's need, and to describe the product properly, using the most appropriate combination of the six specification types. Individual customers, e.g. for consumer goods, are usually incapable of describing and specifying products that will meet their needs.

Earlier in this chapter it was stated that one of the principal quality objectives was "to supply products to customers that conform to their requirements". It has now been argued that these requirements are defined in six different types of manufacturing and quality-control specifications. A vendor who wishes to supply customers with products with which they will be pleased must, unless he is content to rely on good luck, fulfil two requirements. First, his marketing and design people must decide on the product that is to be sold and decide which balance of the six specification types is best able to describe the product and control its conformance. Secondly, the manufacturing people must manufacture a product that conforms to the product description. The task of the quality-control people is to ensure that the two requirements of product description and manufacturing conformance are met by the marketing, design and manufacturing groups who bear the primary responsibility.

POLICIES FOR QUALITY

Every company has a quality policy. In some companies this is decided by the top management and is explicitly stated and communicated to every employee. It is also known to the suppliers and customers of the company. In other companies there is no explicit statement of quality policy, but the employees know that the management does not treat quality as a matter of major importance. They know that any quality decision will be decided by short-term advantage, that manufacturing is entirely output-directed and that loss of market share will be countered by extra advertising. In other companies the management has an ill-defined but positive feeling towards quality, often based on a past reputation, but the real quality policy is set by innumerable operators, inspectors, testers and supervisors each individually deciding how well to make the product and what to accept and reject.

In the writer's own company, International Telephone and Telegraph Corporation, the quality policy is established by the President, H. S. Geneen, and the board of the company. The policy is to supply products and services that:

> Perform exactly like the requirement . . . or cause the requirement to be officially changed to what we and our customers really need.

The writer believes that this is the kind of quality policy that all companies need. This is not because it is a morally right policy—though it undoubtedly is and this is a by no means negligible consideration in a time when the ethical basis of business is being increasingly questioned. It is because analysis suggests and experience confirms that for a company to decide exactly what product it intends to sell, and then to take the steps to make that product exactly, is the most cost-effective way for it to organize its operations. Any quality policy that is half-hearted about complete conformance leads frequently to serious customer reaction and then to expensive and ineffective remedial action. The final costs are then higher than they would have been if a decision had been made at the start to achieve a conforming product and the resulting disruption of production prevents schedules being achieved and delivery dates met. At worst market share is irretrievably lost.

The above does not mean, however, that the quality policy should be to aim for the ultimate in technical performance or aesthetic elegance. (These may be aims of a legitimate marketing policy for some kinds of luxury business.) The quality policy should be to meet exactly a defined requirement.

A major responsibility of top management is to set a company's quality policy and to make sure that every employee knows what that policy is.

2 *Quality Cost Reporting*

It is a generally held view that there is a direct relationship between quality and price. Phrases such as "If you want good quality you must pay for it" are common. It is also widely believed that the price to be paid for perfection must be exceptionally high. Graphs, such as that of Figure 2.1 are given as a means of representing this relationship.

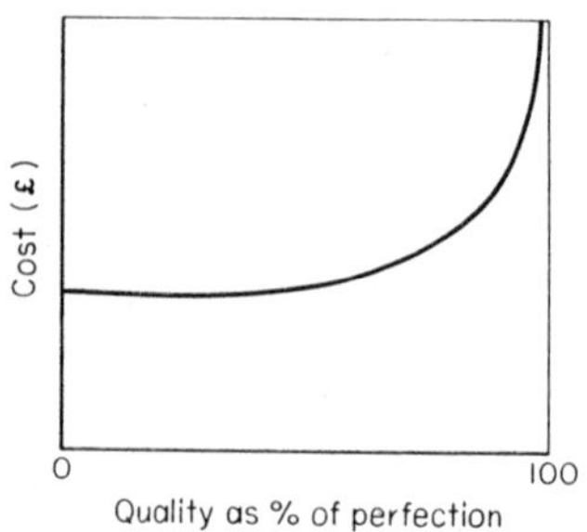

FIGURE 2.1 **Hypothetical relationship between cost and "quality"**

A more sophisticated representation is given in Figure 2.2. Here two graphs are given, one representing the variation in the cost of making a product with different "quality levels" and the other the price that a buyer is prepared to pay for the article. This figure represents the ideas that to make the product at all involves a finite cost, that the cost rises gradually as the quality is improved and that the cost starts to rise steeply as perfection is approached. On the other hand it is suggested that the customer will not be prepared to pay anything for the product if the quality is very bad, but the price obtainable then rises rapidly as the quality improves. However the customer, it is suggested, is not willing to pay excessively for perfection.

According to the adherents of this model a main task of quality control is to get the quality at the "optimum" (near to the dotted line on the figure) where the difference between price and cost is a maximum and profit is highest. Although they have rarely developed the logic thus far, the main ideas of this model are popular with some manufacturing managers. They will agree that the quality must be good enough to be beyond the low-quality loss region: however their chief fear is that the Quality people will force them into the high-quality loss region and their enthusiasm is highest when resisting Quality on these grounds.

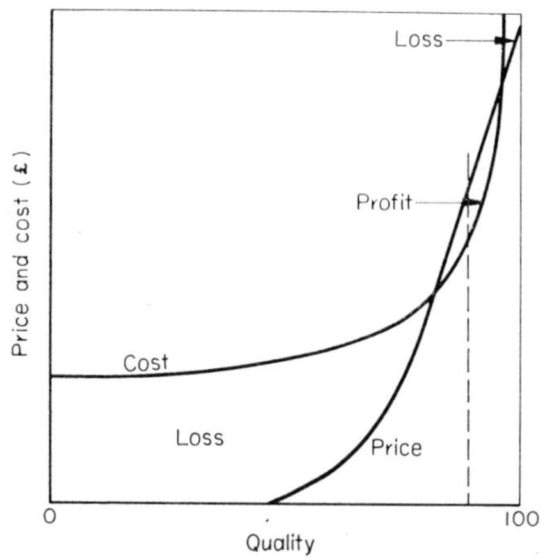

FIGURE 2.2 **Hypothetical relationship between price and cost and "quality"**

The writer's own view is that these hypothetical relationships between quality and price are not very useful. It is true, of course, that each additional performance characteristic specified for a product is likely to add to the cost, and that the cost is likely to rise steeply if the magnitude required for the characteristic approaches the limit of what is technically achievable. (It is therefore very important not to be over-ambitious in specifying the performance of a product.)

One method used in sophisticated, new-product planning is to list all of the possibly required features of the product. Each one of these is given a weighting depending upon its importance and the quantitative levels for excellent, good, fair and poor gradings are established. For example, for a television set several scores of characteristics covering style, appearance, technical performance, features such as push-button control, etc., might be listed and weighted. Different designs (and competitive products) can then be compared quantitatively, those with high ratings being said to have high "quality" and the converse. However, the gradings and weightings depend upon the subjective judgement of the marketing experts making the appraisal and the concept of "perfection" in this context is almost meaningless.

Similar problems arise with the relationship between price and quality (defined in this way). The graph may reasonably express the price that a particular customer may be willing to pay for different levels of performance, etc., but any method of adding together the willingness of a large number of customers must be largely arbitrary.

It has already been argued that for professional quality control the only definition of quality that provides a working tool is "quality means conformance". Using this definition the graphs of Figure 2.2 have the following meaning. Making a product which conforms very poorly to the requirement still costs money. Adding extra cost enables much closer conformance to be achieved, but to achieve exact conformance is likely to cost excessively. The customer will not buy a product that conforms poorly, but is satisfied with "reasonable" conformance, and is not prepared to pay the very high price of perfect conformance.

This reasoning is based on the fallacious idea that the achievement of perfection must take the ultimate in effort and cost. If perfection is taken to be the ultimate integration of all desirable performance and other characteristics this may be so. However, where perfection is simply taken as exact conformance to some clearly specified requirements, this is not so. For most simple items there is no special difficulty in achieving perfection. Most nuts and screws, 1 per cent resistors and bottles of vodka conform exactly to their specifications and can therefore be said to be perfect. More complicated things can easily be made perfect if their requirement is only to meet some clear performance specification that can be tested in a defined way. If the product passes the test it is perfect; if it fails it is re-worked until it is perfect (i.e. passes the test).

The purpose of the last paragraph has not been to argue that it is always easy to achieve perfection, but only to assert that perfection can reasonably be thought of as exact conformance to a specified requirement and that this is not necessarily exceptionally difficult to achieve. There are usually many different ways of making a product, even a properly defined product, and each method will have a different cost. For example, it will invariably cost more to make a product that initially does not conform to its requirements and then test and re-work it, than to make it perfectly (i.e. conforming) the first time.

The conclusion of this section is that, while every required performance characteristic is likely to add cost, exact conformance to the requirements should be a principal aim of the quality-control system.

DEFINITION AND CATEGORIZATION OF QUALITY COSTS

One method of making, inspecting and testing a product is indicated in the flow chart given in Figure 2.3 (there are many others—this is given for the purposes of this section). Purchased parts arrive in the factory and are 100 per cent inspected against the purchasing specifications. The conforming parts are used to make sub-assemblies and non-conforming parts are returned to the supplier. The sub-assemblies are inspected 100 per cent against the sub-assembly specifications and conforming sub-assemblies are used to make the final equipment. Defective sub-assemblies are scrapped. The equipment is 100 per cent tested against the equipment-performance specification and conforming equipment is dispatched to the customer. Defective equipment is re-worked and re-tested. Equipment returned as defective by the customer is also re-worked, re-tested, and returned to the customer.

In Figure 2.4 the re-work cycle is shown in more detail. The equipment test serves the purposes of identifying which equipment conforms to specification and which is defective, and enables the conforming equipment to be available for dispatch to the customer. However, the defective equipment has to be submitted to a further stage of 100 per cent inspection and test (often called fault-finding). In this the individual defect or defects which make each particular equipment defective must be identified. The method of re-work may then be obvious, but in other cases a decision may need to be made, e.g. by a "material-review board", whether or not the equipment can be re-worked, or whether it must be scrapped. Development and industrial engineers may have to be involved in determining the corrective action needed to restore the equipment to a conforming state.

A start can be made in defining quality costs by consideration of the flow charts of Figures 2.3 and 2.4. In general terms quality costs can be defined as follows.

Quality costs are costs associated with making defective product. For service industries "*making defective product*" can be replaced by "*providing defective service*".

All quality costs fall into one of four categories and each of these can be defined precisely. The first two are defined as follows:

(i) *the costs of identifying defective items and separating them from conforming items;*
(ii) *the costs of replacing defective items with conforming items.*

All the boxes in Figures 2.3 and 2.4 except for "incoming parts", "make sub-assemblies", "make equipment" and "dispatch to customer" describe actions whose costs fall into the above two categories.

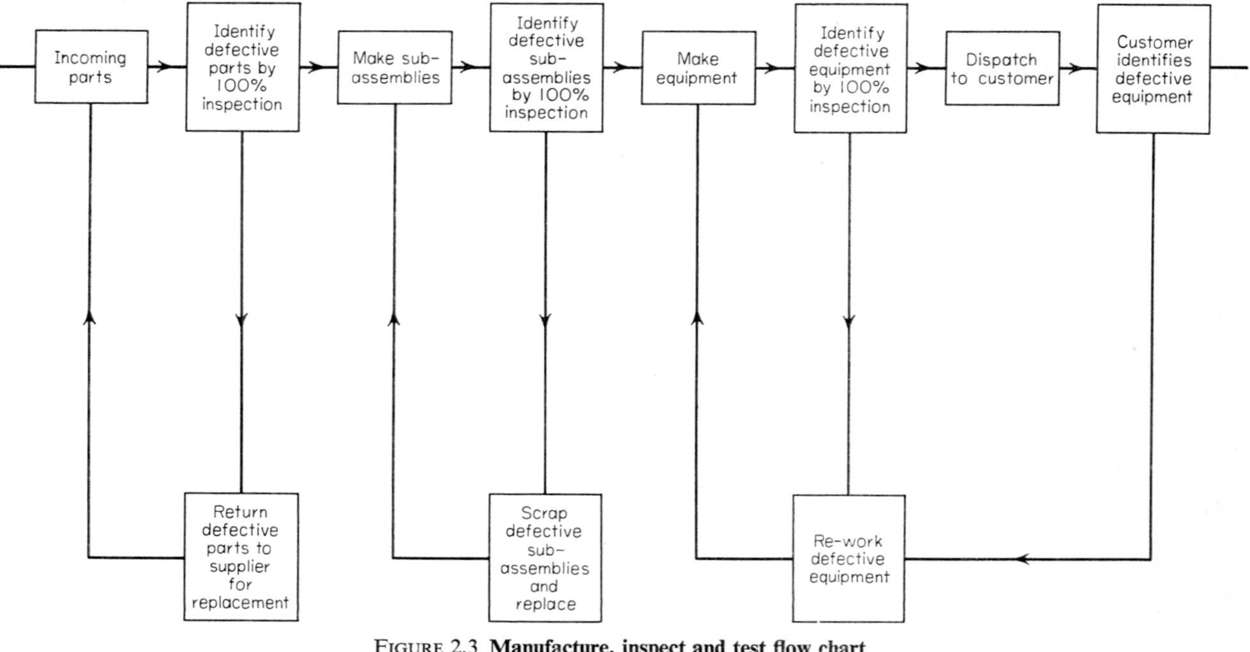

FIGURE 2.3 **Manufacture, inspect and test flow chart**

Defect-prevention activities, which are a major concern of quality control, are deliberately excluded from this chart.

In Figure 2.3 the following boxes:

(i) Identify defective parts by 100 per cent inspection;
(ii) Identify defective sub-assemblies by 100 per cent inspection;
(iii) Identify defective equipment by 100 per cent test;
(iv) Customer identifies defective equipment;

are all actions whose costs are covered by the definition, "the costs of identifying defective items and separating them from conforming items". Box (iv) above will not necessarily result in a quality cost to the producer:[1] this will depend upon the warranty agreement.

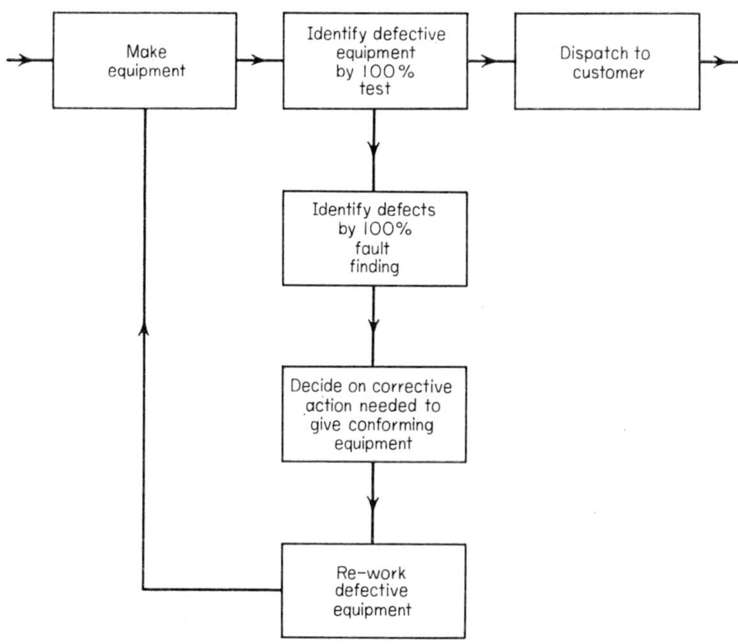

FIGURE 2.4 **Re-work flow chart**

[1] Whether the cost of a particular action is categorized as a quality cost or not depends upon the action, but it also depends upon whose quality costs are being measured. Here quality costs are examined from the viewpoint of the producer of the equipment and not from the viewpoint of the vendors of parts used by the producer or by the latter's customers (see page 27).

The other boxes in Figures 2.3 and 2.4:

(i) Return defective parts to supplier for replacement;
(ii) Scrap defective sub-assemblies and replace;
(iii) Identify defects by 100 per cent fault finding;
(iv) Decide on corrective action needed to give conforming equipment;
(v) Re-work defective equipment;

are all actions whose cost falls within the definition "the costs of replacing defective items with conforming items". Box (i) may not result in cost to the equipment producer: it depends upon the agreement with the vendor. For box (ii) it is assumed that the sub-assemblies cannot be re-worked and must be scrapped. The scrapped sub-assemblies must be replaced and the quality cost of this scrap is equal to the cost of the replacement parts. Boxes (iii) and (iv) cover the re-work of defective equipment. First the defects must be found by 100 per cent fault-finding, then the needed corrective action must be determined and then the defects must be removed by a re-work operation. Where the re-work arises as a result of the customer finding defective equipment the cost to the producer will depend upon the nature of the warranty agreement with the customer.

In Figures 2.3 and 2.4 it was assumed that the various inspections and tests were done on every item, part, sub-assembly and equipment, i.e. 100 per cent inspection or test. Very often the cost can be reduced by doing an inspection or test by sampling instead of 100 per cent. Figure 2.5 shows how one part of Figure 2.3 is modified when sampling is used. The sub-assemblies are collected into lots, which might be 1,000 sub-assemblies or half a day's production or some other convenient grouping. Instead of inspecting each lot 100 per cent a sample is taken from the lot and only the sub-assemblies in the sample are inspected. If the defective level in the sample is less than a specified number the lot as a whole is passed and the sub-assemblies are used for making equipment. If, however, the sample contains more than the specified number of defectives, the lot as a whole is rejected. Under these circumstances all of the sub-assemblies in the lot would not usually be scrapped. The defective lots would be inspected 100 per cent and the defective sub-assemblies identified. These would then be separated from the conforming sub-assemblies and the latter would be passed into a new lot. Often a sample would be taken from the screened lot and this would be inspected to check that the 100 per cent screening had been performed correctly.

It is clear that sampling inspection used in this way has the purpose of "identifying defective items and separating them from conforming items". The costs of this type of sampling inspection therefore fall within the first of our categories of quality costs.

It is seen that the two categories of quality costs:

(i) the costs of identifying defective items and separating them from conforming items; and

(ii) the costs of replacing defective items with conforming items;

embrace many types of inspection and test, both sampling and 100 per cent, fault-finding, scrap, re-work and the costs of corrective action directed at restoring the product to a conforming state.

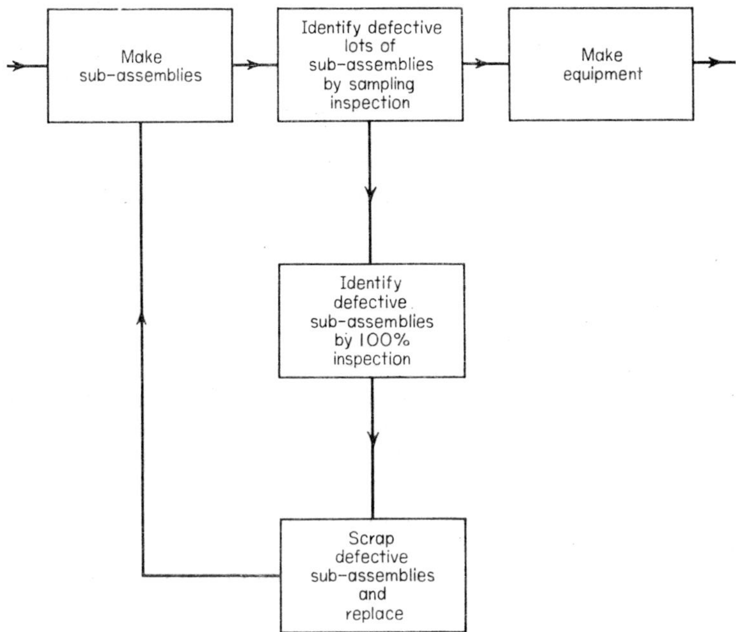

FIGURE 2.5 **Lot-sampling flow chart**

None of the actions whose costs are embraced by these two categories of quality costs are directed towards future improvement. Even the corrective-action investigation preceding re-work has the purpose of finding how best to re-work the already defective product. It is not concerned with improving the method of manufacture, so that, if the product is made again in the future, the same defects will not be produced and there will be no need for re-work.

Trying to improve the manufacturing quality-control system so that in the future it works better than in the present, adds two further categories of quality costs to those discussed above:

(iii) *the costs of trying to prevent the production of defective items;*

(iv) *the cost of trying to improve the effectiveness or reduce the costs of identifying defective items and separating them from conforming items.*

As noted in Chapter 1 the quality system has two main objectives: ensuring that the product as supplied to the customer conforms to its requirements and reducing quality costs. Categories (iii) and (iv) cover actions directed at both these objectives: they are not only concerned with quality-cost reduction. Nevertheless they are closely related to attempts to reduce the quality costs of the first two categories.

Category (iii), the costs of trying to prevent the production of defective items, embraces a large number of activities. First there are all the activities prior to the introduction of a new product such as design review, qualification-testing and vendor survey. Then there are activities which are applied to a running product line, such as defect-reporting and analysis and preventive corrective action. For a running product line those activities which are directed at future improvement must be differentiated from similar activities in defect-detailing, fault-finding and corrective action, which have the aim of getting the current product into a state of conformance. Finally, there are general activities such as operator-quality certification, zero-defect programmes, quality-status reporting, and quality-cost reporting, which have the purpose of training, motivating or aiding members of the company towards the achievement of their quality objectives.

In category (iv) are included such activities as the planning and specification of inspection and test, the application of work-study methods to inspection and test, the training of inspectors and testers, the evaluation and development of new test and inspection equipment, the maintenance and calibration of test equipment, etc.

The design and development of a new product is usually an iterative process in which models and prototypes are tested and their deficiencies determined. Development is then carried further in order to overcome the deficiencies. Most of the costs of this process within the development department should be considered as essential development costs and should not be included in the quality-cost total. For the design and development of a new product only the costs of formal, new-product quality-control procedures such as the participation of quality engineers in design reviews and formal qualification-testing as a means of release for production should be included in quality costs. These latter costs fall within the category of "trying to prevent the production of defective items".

For products in production, design changes can give rise to quality costs. Design changes can be made for several reasons: for cost reduction; to extend the range of purchasable components; because a customer changes his requirements; because Marketing judge sales will be increased, etc. The costs of changes made for reasons of this sort are not quality costs. However, design changes are often made to products in production because the product, as originally designed, did not conform to all of its requirements, i.e. product made according to the design was defective. The extra costs to the manufacturing, installation and quality departments because the product was introduced into production before its design met the requirements are quality costs. These costs include those for scrapping or re-working materials, components sub-assemblies and equipments which were bought or made to the incorrect design. The costs of extra inspection and test will, of course, be included. The costs of the effort that production control, purchasing, industrial engineering, etc., wasted on the wrong design should also be included. All of these are costs of "replacing defective items with conforming items".

In the main, the costs to the design and development department of design changes should not be included in the quality costs. They are merely resuming the development process after they thought they had finished it. However, if it suffers extra costs because it completed the design in two parts, rather than continuously, these costs should be included. If two sets of manufacturing drawings were issued, for example, then the costs of the first, incorrect set would be a quality cost.

In summary, all costs which are classified as quality costs are covered by the four categories:

(i) *Screening:* the costs of identifying defective items and separating them from conforming items.

(ii) *Replacement of defectives:* the costs of replacing defective items with conforming items.

(iii) *Prevention of defectives:* the costs of trying to prevent the production of defective items.

(iv) *Improvement of screening:* the costs of trying to improve the effectiveness or reduce the costs of identifying defective items and separating them from conforming items.

PREVENTION, APPRAISAL AND FAILURE QUALITY COSTS

Quality costs have been customarily divided into the three categories of prevention, appraisal and failure. Failure embraces scrap, re-work and warranty costs, appraisal includes inspection and test, and prevention all the miscellaneous preventive quality activities. In the classification discussed in the first part of this chapter emphasis was given to the purpose of various activities, If, for example, the purpose of an action was to help replace an identified defective item with a conforming item, then the costs of the action were included as quality costs in the category of "replacement of defectives". The action might be an inspection to detail the defects needing re-work, or it might be an assembly operation re-working the item or some other type of action.

In the conventional division into prevention, appraisal and failure, on the other hand, there is less emphasis on the purpose of actions. This is most apparent in the appraisal category, which includes all inspection and test, irrespective of purpose. Inspection and test is obviously often done with the purpose of identifying defective items—"screening"—but it is also done as a means of enabling defective items to be re-worked—"replacement of defectives"—and as a means of providing defect information which on analysis is used to help to prevent the production of similar defective items in the future, i.e. "prevention of defectives". Inspection and test also includes some activities which do not fall within any of the four categories of quality cost, such as the adjustment during test of variable controls (this happens, for example, during the testing of television sets). In the writer's view, these costs are not properly quality costs, but for convenience they are sometimes included in the appraisal costs.

It is seen that the conventional category of appraisal costs, because it includes all inspection and test costs, embraces all screening costs and also some of the costs of replacing defectives and some of the costs of preventing defectives.

The prevention category then includes all remaining costs associated with preventing the production of defectives and improving screening. The failure category includes all remaining costs of replacing defectives.

The major advantage of the conventional method of categorizing quality costs is that it makes the accounting easy. All inspection and test costs are placed in appraisal and it is unnecessary to decide for reporting purposes whether the purpose of a particular test or inspection was for screening, or as an aid to re-work of a defective or in order to help prevent future defectives. It must be emphasized that the only difference between the conventional categorization and the logical breakdown given at the start of this chapter is in the transfer of some of the quality costs from one category to another.

There is no difference in definition of what are and are not quality costs.

The failure category is also sometimes subdivided into internal failures and external failures. External-failure costs include costs, such as warranty costs, of which the customer has direct knowledge and for which he often makes a direct charge. Internal-failure costs include costs, such as scrap and re-work, of which the customer is unaware. This separation is useful because, for reasons which are explained later in this chapter, external-failure costs are more serious than internal-failure costs.

Yet another method of categorizing quality costs is sometimes attempted. Here the emphasis is put not on the purpose of the activities leading to quality costs, nor on the activities themselves, but on different groups of people within the company. The titles prevention, appraisal and failure are used, but, for example, the appraisal costs are categorized as costs within the responsibility of the quality department and failure costs as costs within the responsibility of the production department. It is then argued that the costs of re-inspection and re-test of product which has been re-worked should be counted as failure costs, because the need for re-inspection and re-test was the fault of the production department.

In the writer's view it is undesirable to categorize quality costs in this way for three reasons:

(i) it is very difficult to determine quantitatively and completely the groups actually responsible for causing particular quality costs and the attempt makes the accounting excessively difficult;

(ii) effective reduction of most of the quality-cost categories requires co-operative action from a number of departments and this is hindered if departments are encouraged to think some of the categories are none of their responsibility;

(iii) the method of categorization does not lead to any logical definition of quality costs.

Sub-categories of Quality Costs

It is useful to break down the main prevention, appraisal and failure categories of quality costs into further sub-categories. These sub-categories can be varied to suit particular circumstances and should be such that the trade-off between accounting difficulty and the needs of control is optimized. One set of sub-categories that is based on the system used in ITT is given in Table 2.1:

TABLE 2.1

Sub-categories of Quality Costs

1 *Prevention Costs*
- 1.1 Pre-production quality control
- 1.2 Vendor quality control
- 1.3 Inspection and test planning
- 1.4 Design and development of inspection and test equipment
- 1.5 Quality training
- 1.6 Quality system audits

2 *Appraisal Costs*
- 2.1 Incoming test and inspection
- 2.2 In-process and final test and inspection
- 2.3 Installation test and inspection
- 2.4 Test and inspection equipment
- 2.5 Maintenance and calibration of test and inspection equipment
- 2.6 Product-quality audits

3 *Failure Costs*
- 3.1 Scrap (Manufacturing)
- 3.2 Re-work (Manufacturing)
- 3.3 Scrap (Installation)
- 3.4 Re-work (Installation)
- 3.5 Complaints and warranty

COMPTROLLER RESPONSIBILITY FOR QUALITY-COST MEASURING

The actual measurement of quality costs is the responsibility of the comptroller department, not the quality department. There are several reasons for this. First, the comptroller's department is responsible for measuring all other costs, so this precedent should be followed unless there are good reasons to the contrary. Secondly, the quality department shares the responsibility for controlling and reducing quality costs and it is bad, in principle, for a department to measure and report its own success or failure, without independent check. Thirdly, top management is used to getting its cost information from the comptroller's department and will take more seriously information from this source. If the comptroller department will not measure quality costs the reason is that the comptroller has not been convinced that it is important to do so. The quality manager may be able to present to him the necessary arguments. A more effective way is for the general manager to tell the comptroller that he wants quality costs reported. If this is said with conviction it leads to a rapid solution of any technical accounting difficulties.

The main failure costs (see Table 2.1) are scrap, re-work and warranty. Measurement of scrap and re-work costs requires a system of scrap and re-work tickets. These are raised by Production foremen to cover the extra material and labour required and are passed to the comptroller's department for overhead to be added and for the totals to be made. For scrap and re-work the definition, "the cost of replacing defective items by conforming items" is applicable. If a sub-assembly is scrapped the applicable quality cost is the cost to replace the scrapped sub-assembly by a conforming sub-assembly. Similarly, if an equipment must be re-worked the applicable quality cost is the total cost to get the defective equipment into conformance. When this has been done the defective equipment has, in effect, been replaced by a conforming equipment. Where a standard cost system is in use the scrap and re-work costs will include material, labour and overhead. For a standard cost system it will be usual to have reporting of scrap and re-work even in the absence of a quality-cost reporting system. This is because scrap and re-work are important constituents of manufacturing cost variances. Sometimes an allowance for scrap and/or re-work is included in the standard cost. The manufacturing variances will then include only the scrap and re-work variances from standard. However, for quality-cost reporting it is important that the total scrap and re-work is included, otherwise the quality costs will be seriously understated.

For warranty costs the actual costs paid to the customer must be included. Costs should not be excluded because they are in respect of product made in previous financial years, although it is desirable for large costs to indicate this on the reporting document. High warranty costs from previous years can give a powerful incentive for due weight to be given to the reliability of current product.

The main costs in the prevention and appraisal categories are the costs of people: inspectors, testers, quality engineers, test-equipment development engineers, etc. The greatest difficulty in measuring these quality costs concerns overheads. For manufacturing operations using a standard cost system many of the people engaged in prevention and appraisal activities will be categorized as indirect. This means that their costs are already completely absorbed in the overhead applied to the direct production operators. The assessment of the overhead to be applied to these people for quality-cost purposes obviously presents problems. On the other hand many of the inspectors and testers may be categorized as direct with an automatic standard-cost overhead applied to their labour costs. One method of reporting prevention and appraisal costs, which has the advantage of accounting simplicity, is to include direct inspectors and testers at their loaded rate, but for indirect staff to give only salaries. This has a number of objections of which the most important are, first that the reported quality costs will be increased if any inspection jobs are re-categorized from indirect to direct (even though the duties performed and the actual quality costs are unchanged) and, secondly, that comparison of quality costs of different units will be hampered if they have different practices with regard to direct and indirect categorization. Another method of treating prevention and appraisal quality costs is to report only the wages or salaries of all staff concerned, irrespective of whether they are categorized direct or indirect. This again has the advantage of simplicity and may be an acceptable first step towards a good reporting system. The main objection is that it gives a serious understatement of the quality costs.

The best method of treating overheads in prevention and appraisal quality costs is to report the wages and salaries of all inspectors, testers and other quality staff and to add all the extra costs of these people. The costs reported are independent of whether staff are categorized as direct or indirect. These include all the personal cost such as social-security costs, holiday pay, etc., costs of travelling, entertaining, etc., costs to cover the floor space they occupy, heat, lighting, telephones, etc., costs of services from other departments, e.g. personnel, costs of tools. The costs of test and inspection equipment need special consideration. For maintenance and calibration the costs reported are simply those of the engineers and technicians treated as described earlier in this paragraph. The cost of test and inspection equipment in use should be given as a depreciation cost, and this cost can either be reported in a separate sub-section (2.4 in Table 2.1) or can be added in to the costs of the various test and inspection groups using the equipment. The costs of groups developing and making test and inspection equipment should be included, but the value of equipment they produce, which is to be capitalized and subsequently depreciated, should be deducted.

The proper treatment of costs, other than salaries and wages, in the prevention and appraisal categories is of major importance in quality-cost reporting. The overhead costs as described in the previous paragraph are likely to approach 100 per cent of the wage and salary quality costs and may be 20 to 30 per cent of the total quality costs.

One other point is of major importance in reporting appraisal costs. The costs of all staff engaged in "identifying defective items and separating them from conforming items" must be included in the appraisal costs irrespective of organization. 100 per cent screening operations carried out by members of the production department or tests carried out by an installation group result in quality costs just as do the actions of members of the quality department. Similarly, "detailing" of the reasons for rejection in order to facilitate re-work is a quality cost whether done by inspection or production. However, it may be convenient in the one case to report it as an appraisal cost and in the other as a re-work cost, and this is acceptable provided that reporting is done consistently. Finally, some activities of the quality department should be excluded from quality-cost reporting. This applies when for organizational reasons the quality department is responsible for non-quality activities, e.g. the storekeeping aspects of controlling a bonded store, or responsibilities for packaging and shipping, or goods-inwards activities.

THE PURPOSES OF QUALITY-COST REPORTING

Having defined quality costs and shown how they are measured and reported it is now the place to discuss the purposes of quality-cost reporting. Most companies do not measure their quality costs explicitly and this shows that quality-cost measurement is not needed for essentially financial purposes—for deriving the profit or loss of the company, for setting the dividend or paying the taxes. The inspection, test and quality-control costs are included in the direct or indirect manufacturing costs, the scrap and re-work costs are included in the standard costs or appear as variances and the warranty costs are included as a marketing expense. The purposes of collecting together the separate quality costs and reporting them are not financial; they are concerned with management control.

For a company that is divided into a number of separate units for management control the purposes of quality-cost reporting in a unit can be listed as follows:

(i) to enable the unit's managers to know the size of their quality-cost problem so that they can apply appropriate resources to its solution;

(ii) to show broadly where the problem is, e.g. in inspection or in warranty, so that unit management can concentrate effort effectively;

(iii) to enable unit management to set targets for quality-cost reduction and to plan actions to meet the targets;

(iv) to enable progress towards meeting the targets to be measured;

(v) to enable company management to motivate unit management to set ambitious targets and to provide help to unit management for their achievement.

It will be shown later that quality costs are an important part of total manufacturing costs. It is a management axiom that it is difficult to control anything that is not being measured. Quality-cost measuring and reporting is an essential tool for the control and reduction of quality costs and perhaps the chief purpose of quality-cost reporting is to motivate management to control these costs.

Quality-cost Indices

All the purposes of quality-cost reporting cannot be met merely by reporting total quality costs in pounds sterling or even by showing how the total is divided into different categories. Quality costs of £100,000 per annum could be the most important problem of a small unit but be of minor importance to a unit ten times as large. A unit's management might target to reduce its quality costs by 10 per cent in a year and find at the end of the year, despite energetic action on defect prevention, that its quality costs had risen not fallen—because the unit's sales had increased by a very desirable 20 per cent.

The means of overcoming these problems is to express quality costs as a ratio to some financial measure of a unit's level of activity. There are many such measures: sales, added value, shop cost, standard cost, gross margin, etc. In principle there is no reason why quality cost should not be given as a ratio to all of these bases and more, or at least to such of them as are readily available from normal financial reporting. However, such complication is more likely to confuse management than assist them in taking correct action in quality-cost control. For simplicity it is best to use one or at most two bases.

The most generally used base for quality costs is sales. Sales has the great advantage of being understood, as a measure of a unit's activity, by all managers. It needs no explanation or definition. A change in the quality-cost to sales ratio can immediately be converted into an effect on the unit's profitability. If the quality-cost to sales ratio falls in successive years from 10 per cent to 9 per cent, the effect must be a 1 per cent improvement in the ratio of net profit to sales (there is nowhere that a real reduction in quality-costs can go except on to the net profit). The profit to sales ratio is one of the most important indices of a unit's financial success, so its close relationship to the quality-cost to sales ratio gives another reason for favouring sales as a base in quality-cost reporting.

However sales also has important disadvantages as a base. For example, some management units may not make sales. Individual factories may transfer their product at cost to a central marketing organization. In this circumstance sales cannot be used as a base. Most of the other objections to sales as a base arise from the fact that, of the major quality-cost categories—inspection, test, scrap, re-work and warranty—all but warranty are associated with the manufacturing and installation phases of activity. The main items that comprise sales are given in the following equation:

Sales = cost of purchased material + cost of sub-contracting + added shop cost + added installation cost + gross margin + decrease in inventory

The first four items in the equation comprise the manufacturing/installation cost. For reasons that are explained in the next section, only a small part of the quality costs of a unit's purchased materials and sub-contract activities are recorded in the unit's quality costs. Similarly, gross margin contains only warranty costs and inventory changes have little if any quality-cost content. From this it follows that units which have a high proportion of their sales in added shop cost and/or added installation costs are likely to have a high quality-cost to sales ratio, irrespective of the effectiveness of their quality-cost control procedures. An example of such an operation is the manufacture of transistors where purchases may be only basic matertials such as silicon crystal and the major part of the value is added in the factory. Conversely, re-sale operations will have very low quality-cost to sales ratios, and assembly operations with a large content of purchased component costs and sub-contract costs will have fairly low quality-cost to sales ratios. As an example, a particular assembly operation for television sets had 80 per cent of its manufacturing costs in purchased electronic components, purchased cabinets, etc. The quality cost it spent in controlling the purchased content (incoming inspection, vendor surveys, etc.) was however only one-tenth of the quality cost of inspection, test, re-work, etc., for the 20 per cent of cost added in the factory. Simply as a consequence of this its quality-cost to sales ratio was low.

Any change in the balance of a unit's activities from one year to the next, e.g. as a result of a decision to buy a component rather than make it, or to do more sub-contract work, can markedly affect the quality-cost to sales ratio.

For all these reasons it is useful to use another base as well as (not instead of) sales against which to compare quality costs. It is the writer's opinion that the best additional base is "added shop and installation cost". This can be in terms of standard cost or actual cost.

Remembering that the purpose of quality-cost reporting is to enable planned actions to be taken to reduce quality costs and to be able to measure the effect of these actions, the advantages of added shop and installation cost as the second base for quality costs are:

(i) It is applicable to units that do not make sales (total shop and installation cost would also satisfy this requirement).

(ii) It is relatively little affected by changes in gross margin or the proportion of material purchased. The effect on the quality-cost to added-cost ratio is, in any case, opposite to the effect on the quality-cost to sales ratio. (Increasing the proportion of purchased materials will decrease the quality-cost to sales ratio, but will increase the quality-cost to added-shop cost ratio, because of the extra incoming inspection needed. This enables the effect of a change in the proportion of purchased material to be differentiated from a real quality-cost improvement, owing to preventive corrective action, which has the effect of reducing both ratios.)

(iii) The quality-cost to added-shop-cost ratio is likely to be a high number, perhaps 50 per cent or more, and as such is effective in triggering management action. In the TV-factory example given above, the quality cost as a ratio to total shop cost was only 6 per cent, but to added shop cost it was 30 per cent, a much more dramatic figure.

The two quality-cost indices—ratio to sales and ratio to added shop and installation cost—are particularly useful in assessing the magnitude of the quality-cost problem, in setting targets for quality-cost reduction and for measuring progress against these targets.

An example is used to illustrate the method of target-setting. A particular unit might have sales of £1,000,000 in one year and quality costs of £100,000, the quality-cost to sales ratio being 10 per cent. A simple way of target-setting would be to set a target for quality costs of £90,000 in the next year. However, a better way would be to set the target in terms of the ratio to sales as 9 per cent in the next year. If the sales in the second year remain at £1,000,000 the two methods of targeting give the same result. However, if the sales rise the second method of targeting requires a smaller reduction in quality cost and in this example the target can be achieved with no reductions in quality cost if the sales in the second year rise to £1,111,000. Conversely, if the sales drop the second method of targeting requires a larger reduction of quality cost. This method of target-setting takes account of the realistic situations that inspection, test, scrap and re-work are likely to increase if the activity level increases and must be brought down if the activity level decreases.

This last conclusion is invalidated in so far as there is fixed overhead within the quality costs. Usually, there is insufficient fixed overhead included to make any quantitative estimate of its effect worth while. It is sufficient to remember that the small fixed overhead makes it easier to achieve the quality-cost target if the sales exceed budget and more difficult if sales fall below budget.

It is useful to be able to express the results of a change in quality-cost to sales ratio in terms of money. The way to do this can be illustrated by assuming in our example that in the second year the sales rose to £1,200,000 and the quality-cost to sales ratio fell to the targeted 9 per cent. The change represents a saving in the second year compared to the first of £12,000. If the quality-cost ratio had not improved, the quality costs in the second year would have been 10 per cent of £1,200,000, i.e. £120,000. In fact they were 9 per cent of £1,200,000, i.e. £108,000, giving a saving of £12,000. A saving is recorded even though the actual quality cost in the second year is £8,000 more than in the first year.
The formula to express this relationship is:

$$\text{quality cost saving (year 2) £'s} = \left[\left(\frac{\text{quality cost}}{\text{sales}}\right)_{\text{year 1}} - \left(\frac{\text{quality cost}}{\text{sales}}\right)_{\text{year 2}}\right] \quad \underset{\text{year 2}}{\text{Sales £'s}}$$

The formula can be used to calculate the saving to date during year 2; it is not limited to the year-end figure. In our example the sales in the first four months of year 2 might have been £400,000 and the quality costs £38,000, i.e. 9·5 per cent. Application of the formula gives:

$$\begin{array}{c}\text{quality cost saving} \\ \text{in 4 months (£'s)}\end{array} = £[0{\cdot}1 - 0{\cdot}095]\,400{,}000 = £2{,}000$$

Quality-cost reductions can be targeted and measured in exactly the same way using the quality-cost to added-shop-cost ratio, and this is possibly a more realistic way of targeting, provided all the managers concerned have a clear understanding of what added shop cost is.

WIDER ASPECTS OF QUALITY COSTS

Earlier in this chapter quality costs were defined in a restricted way. This restricted definition is the one of most practical usefulness. It enables quality costs to be measured in a controlled manner and this in turn allows meaningful targets for quality-cost reduction to be established and planned actions for the achievement of the targets to be made. The restrictions made were of two main types. First, a particular manufacturing unit was implicitly assumed and the definition of quality costs was restricted to cover only direct costs to that unit. Indirect costs associated with the unit's vendors and customers were excluded. In the case of vendors this means that costs to the unit of such things as incoming inspection and vendor appraisals carried out by the unit's own staff were included in the measured quality costs. However, the vendors' quality costs were excluded. These might have a marked effect on the price paid by the unit for its purchased materials and parts, but by definition they are not included in the unit's quality costs. As an example, for electronic equipment such as a TV set or an electronic telephone exchange, the electronic components are usually responsible for more than half the total cost of the equipment. Complex electronic components such as transistors, tubes or integrated circuits have high quality costs, often 20 per cent or more of the sales value. In this example therefore the component quality costs will be a significant part of the cost of the whole electronic equipment. However, by definition these quality costs are not included in the quality costs of the unit making the electronic equipment. They are simply "lost" in the cost of the purchased components.

There are practical reasons for this approach such as the virtual impossibility of getting vendors to reveal their quality costs.

The same approach applies with the unit's customers. The quality costs that the customer has to bear as a result of less than perfect conformance of the unit's products are not included in the unit's quality costs, unless, as for example in the case of warranty costs, they are directly charged back to the unit. The costs that the customer bears on the unit's equipment for repair, loss of service during breakdown, provision of standby equipment, etc., are not, by definition, included in the unit's quality costs, unless they are charged directly to the unit.

The phrase "cost of ownership" is used to express the idea that the cost of buying a particular item, even a capital item, will be only a part, and possibly a small part, of the total cost to the purchaser of the item. The operating costs may be of similar magnitude to the initial capital costs. To the customer of the unit, whose quality costs are being measured, the cost of ownership of the unit's products may include large amounts for repair, maintenance, etc. These costs are quality costs to its customer, but are not included in the quality costs of the unit.

As with vendor's quality costs, the reasons for not including the quality costs of customers in a unit's measured quality costs are largely practical: there is usually no way for the unit to measure the quality costs of the customers and to separate out the part of these due to the unit's products.

This fact is of major importance. It means that in practice it is not possible to express the entire quality task of the unit in terms of quality costs. This is why there are two major quality objectives (Chapter 1):

(i) to make products for sale that conform to their requirements;

and

(ii) to minimize quality costs.

If the products sold do not conform to their requirements the assumption is that they will give the customer inferior performance, reliability, maintainability, etc., and that as a consequence the unit's sales will be harmed. (It is also true, of course, that poor judgement of the requirements of the product will harm sales, but this is a failure of marketing and development, not of quality control.) There is no practical way of measuring the magnitude of the effect on sales of different degrees of departure from conformance, and of expressing this magnitude as quality costs. It is therefore essential to establish conformance as a prime quality objective and not only to emphasize minimization of quality costs.

The first way in which practical measurements of quality costs are restricted, it is seen, is because most of the quality costs of a unit's vendors and the quality part of the customer's costs of ownership of the unit's products, are not included. The second way in which practical quality-cost measurements are restricted is because attention is directed at the unit's saleable products. Quality control is concerned with human error and one of the slogans of quality control is "do it right the first time". However, only the costs of errors leading directly to product defects are included in quality costs. It might well be possible to measure the costs of typing errors in the typing pool and book-keeping errors in the accounts department and stock-level errors in the production-control department, and indeed such things are measured during an overall quality-improvement programme. However, their costs are not included in quality costs. Similarly the important human errors in design, marketing and management generally which are probably impossible to quantify are not included. Even with hindsight the judgement of error in these areas must be subjective. The practical approach therefore is to restrict quality-cost reporting to product quality costs. These can be measured objectively and progress, or deterioration assessed with confidence that the figures reflect reality.

3 *Quality Management*

There are a number of questions that must be answered about the organization and functions of the quality department. Is a quality department needed? If so, what functions should it perform? How should it fit into the overall organization of a unit? How should the department itself be organized?

Feigenbaum, in his book *Total Quality Control,*[1] emphasized that quality is everybody's business, but that it is necessary to have a department concerned only with quality. Where such a department did not exist, other departments, development, manufacturing, marketing, etc., were unlikely to give sufficient account to quality and the business as a whole would suffer.

What then are the responsibilities of the quality department? These fall into two main categories. First, it should audit[2] the quality activities of the other departments and report upon them to the department managers and to general management. Secondly, it has direct responsibilities of its own.

In Chapter 1 it was stated that each sale involved a defined product, an agreed price and an agreed delivery time and that an overall business aim was to achieve conformance to all three. For the supplying unit the agreed price requires achievement by the manufacturing department of defined costs. If these are exceeded, profits are reduced or become losses. A major function of the comptroller's department is to measure the product costs of the manufacturing department and to highlight to the management of the unit any important variations from standard. It is not a responsibility of the comptroller's depart-

[1] McGraw-Hill, 1961.

[2] The word "audit" is here used in the sense of an appraisal of activities; it is also used in a different manner concerned with the assessment of product quality (see Chapter 6).

ment to reduce manufacturing costs or adverse cost variances—although it may make suggestions—but it is a responsibility of this department to ensure that the manufacturing manager and the general manager are in no doubt about the cost position, and also to motivate them to improve.

In a similar way, a major responsibility of the quality department is to audit and report on the quality performance of other departments and to motivate them to improve. In many ways this task is more complex and difficult than the comptroller's. The latter can report cost variances directly in money terms, and the unit's managers can immediately estimate the effect of these variances on profit. The quality manager can rarely express the quality position directly and completely in money terms and the effect of inadequate product conformance on profit is indirect and delayed in time. There is no dispute that it is a responsibility of the comptroller to report cost variances, and the methods of doing this are stereotyped. For these reasons the comptroller usually escapes the odium that is often received by the bearer of bad news. The quality manager may not be so fortunate.

The activities of other departments which the quality department should audit are those which affect the conformance to requirements of the product offered for sale or the quality costs.

The quality responsibilities of the marketing department include a precise description of the required characteristics of new products and participation with the design/development department in the accurate specification of new products. They also include proper attention to the aspects of contracts concerned with product specifications and customer acceptance procedures.

For the design/development department quality responsibilities include complete product and process specifications (defining what the product should be, what it should do and how it should be made). Auxiliary to this is the provision of efficient systems to control the configuration of the product. Each unit of product should be made to a defined set of drawings or specifications and this in turn requires that the design/development department must have a properly constituted section to control the release of drawings and specifications and to control changes to these. The design/development department is responsible for instituting design-review procedures and also has responsibilities with regard to product qualification and re-qualification.

The manufacturing department is responsible for ensuring that process specifications are adhered to, that parts, sub-assemblies and equipment are manufactured using tools and machines that enable the product specifications to be met and that operators are selected and trained to a level of skill that enables conforming product to be made. The manufacturing department is responsible for making the product in conformance to its requirements first time.

The purchasing department is responsible for selecting vendors and sub-contractors who are capable of supplying parts and materials conforming to specifications and controlling these vendors so that they do. The comptroller department is responsible for measuring and reporting the unit's quality costs in an accurate and clear manner.

All departments are responsible for participating in formalized defect-prevention activities.

Listed above are some of the activities of several departments which are important for product quality and quality costs and which the quality department should audit. Many of these activities will be described in detail in other chapters.

In addition to these auditing and reporting responsibilities, the quality department has direct responsibilities of its own. Many of these concern inspection and test. All inspection and test should be carried out by the quality department. The reasons for this and circumstances in which alternative arrangements may be applicable will be discussed later in this chapter. By inspection is meant all activities whereby purchased materials and parts, manufactured parts and sub-assemblies and finished products are inspected to see if they are what the relevant drawings and specifications say they should be, and by test is meant activities to check that these items perform as specified.

The quality department is also responsible for the support activities that enable inspection and test to be carried out efficiently. These are usually called inspection and test planning (or quality planning). Inspection planning includes preparing documentation, based on engineering drawings and specifications that define to the inspectors exactly how they shall carry out all the inspection operations and the stages within the production process at which inspection will be performed. It also includes procuring, either by buying or by specifying and ordering from the tool shop, necessary inspection gauges and jigs.

Test planning includes similar activities with regard to test. For advanced products, however, test planning may need a high level of technical expertise comparable with that required by development engineering. The required test equipment may not be obtainable on the market and test planning will then include the definition and specification of the test-equipment requirements. The test-planning activity, together with purchasing, will work with test-equipment manufacturers to obtain the required equipment. Test-planning groups are often involved in the development and manufacture of special-purpose test equipment. To some extent this is both inevitable and desirable. However, it is an activity that the quality manager must limit. Test-planning groups, if left to themselves, can become involved in major test-equipment developments, without being subjected to the disciplines that apply to the development and manufacture of the unit's own products. Wherever possible test equipment should be bought and, where this is not possible, major developments should be sub-contracted to an engineering department. For advanced automatic test equipment test planning includes the responsibility for converting the primary engineering into test programmes, i.e. preparing the paper tape or computer programmes. An associated responsibility of the quality department is for the systematic calibration of test and inspection equipment.

Another main group of direct activities of the quality department is concerned with preventing the production of defective product. There are three main areas for work of this kind. For most manufacturing companies the purchase of materials and parts and subcontracting are major activities. The quality-department responsibilities for these items will be discussed in Chapter 7. The second area concerns new products and this will be discussed in Chapter 8. The third concerns the prevention of the production of defective product in the manufacturing phase. All of these activities are customarily included as part of quality engineering.

The last main group of direct activities of the quality department involve co-operation with the training department in quality training. This includes training of quality-department staff, inspectors, testers, quality planners and quality engineers, assessment of the quality performance of newly trained production operators and the training of members of other departments from senior managers to unskilled operators, in an understanding of quality.

The direct responsibilities of the quality department include inspection, test, quality planning, defect-prevention activities (quality engineering) and quality training. These are additional to its responsibility for auditing and reporting upon the quality activities of other departments.

QUALITY PROBLEM SOLVING

When the management of a company becomes aware (often as a result of customer reaction) that it needs to give greater attention to product quality, a common reaction is to set up a small quality-engineering group. The responsibilities of the group may not be well defined and because of immediate pressures it quickly finds that its time is devoted largely to "fixing quality problems". The same is often true of the quality-engineering sections of long-established quality departments. If the quality engineers are technically competent they may give some alleviation of the unit's problems, but they are most unlikely to produce the dramatic improvement obtainable by an effective quality-improvement programme (see Chapter 4), and, as their time is devoted to problem-solving, it cannot be devoted to organized quality improvement.

A good rule for management to apply is that *there are no quality problems*. The reasons for applying this rule are that the phrase "quality problem" is inexplicit and gives no indication of the cause of the problem. It also suggests that the problem is the fault of the quality department and that it (through its quality engineers) should be responsible for solving it. Instead of using the phrase "quality problem" it is better to speak of "conformance problem". This, at least, makes it clear that the problem is that in some respect the product does not conform to its requirements. The cause is usually a deficiency of either manufacturing or engineering. Once this is defined (and the quality engineers should help in this) the group responsible for solving the problem is clarified. Sometimes a failing of an inspection or test section causes the problem. Of course, if the product had been designed and manufactured properly the first time, errors of inspection or test would not affect the level of product conformance; however, this is not a fair assessment of responsibility in cases where, for example, a piece of test equipment is allowed to go out of calibration or a poorly trained inspector applies a wrong standard. Whenever possible it is better to speak, not of a conformance problem, but of a manufacturing problem, a design problem, an inspection problem or a test problem. A description of this kind means that the first step in solving the problem has been made: the group which caused the problem has been determined and first responsibility for its solution has been assigned. An important responsibility of quality engineering is to establish systems so that problems of non-conformance are observed quickly, the people who are doing something wrongly are made aware of it in a clear manner, and they are motivated to carry out corrective actions and these actions are audited.

It is wrong for quality engineers to have conformance problem solving as their main task. It stops them working effectively on defect prevention. It also allows Manufacturing to escape responsibility for solving manufacturing problems and Engineering for solving design problems (and usually, if they try, these departments are better able to solve their problems than quality engineering). Finally, it commits Quality to particular solutions of problems. They are then no longer objective in reporting—members of the quality department may accept non-conformant product, because they are unable to come up with a method of solving the conformance problem and they think it is their responsibility to do so.

In the situation where Quality has accepted responsibility for solving problems it is difficult to make a change. Manufacturing may not have built up the technical competence to solve its problems; Engineering may feel that only new developments are its responsibility. Most important, the quality engineers will like solving conformance problems. It is what they are used to doing and what they have become good at. They feel they are "making a real contribution"; they are praised by the manufacturing department as "members of the team." To drive at defect prevention, to start a design-review system with Engineering, to audit qualification tests, to set up vendor-control and source-inspection systems are some of the things the quality engineers should be doing. However, they are often reluctant to start on these difficult tasks and prefer to continue to spend their time in the solution of "quality problems".

ORGANIZATION OF THE QUALITY DEPARTMENT

There are no firm rules that must be followed in allocating the main quality-department responsibilities of inspection, test, planning, quality engineering, quality training and quality auditing. One typical organization is given in Figure 3.1 but many acceptable variations are possible. Where the unit has two or three well-defined product lines it may be correct to have a combined inspection and test section for each product line. A similar solution may be adopted where the

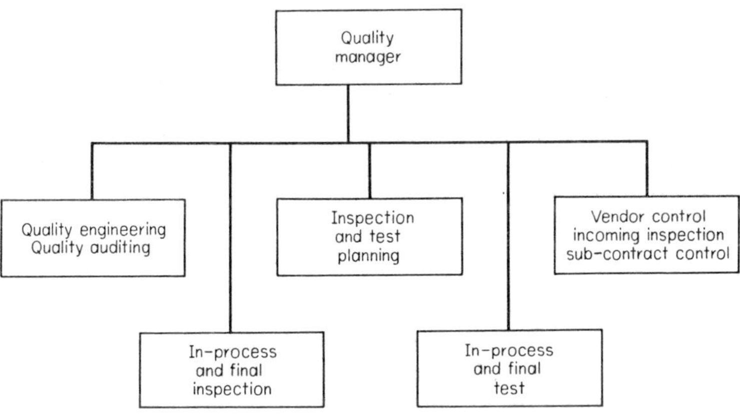

FIGURE 3.1 **Example of quality department organization**

unit has two or more plants at different locations. Of course, the availability of people with particular talents and abilities also influences the organization of the department.

Very often the organization of the quality department owes more to history and expediency than to rational analysis. An inefficient organization often results when management decides to extend the activities of a long-established inspection and test department and appoints a quality manager over the existing chief inspector. This can give an organization exemplified by Figure 3.2.

This structure is not compatible with the "span of control" concept of good organization. The quality manager has three people reporting to him, the chief inspector four and at other levels the reporting number is two or three. The structure is very complicated with too many reporting levels, unnecessary supervisors and poor communications. The quality department is not integrated; all that has happened is that small groups dealing with specialized activities have been grafted on to the existing test and inspection department. As much as nine-tenths of the quality manager's department may be controlled by the chief inspector. Even quality departments having different origins have a tendency to contain too many reporting levels. The ideal is for the quality manager to have five to eight people reporting directly to him and in a small department for this to be the only level of supervision. Larger departments should contain only one additional level.

The Relationship of Inspection, Test, Quality and Manufacturing

One of the two most controversial subjects concerned with the organization of the quality department—the other will be dealt with later in this chapter—deals with the question: Should inspection and test report to Manufacturing or to Quality? The majority of engineers with a manufacturing background—and also many engineers with a quality background—believe that it is better and more efficient for inspection and test to be part of the manufacturing department. The writer believes the opposite: that inspection and test should be part of the quality department. Some of the arguments for the former view and their answers are given below.

"The general manager has got to have one man he can make responsible for output." The ultimate in this argument would be for the general manager to have one man responsible for *everything*: engineering, marketing, manufacturing, the lot. The point is simply one of span of control. In principle, the general manager adds a little to his own work if the manufacturing manager and the quality manager both have some responsibility for output. In practice, it is very

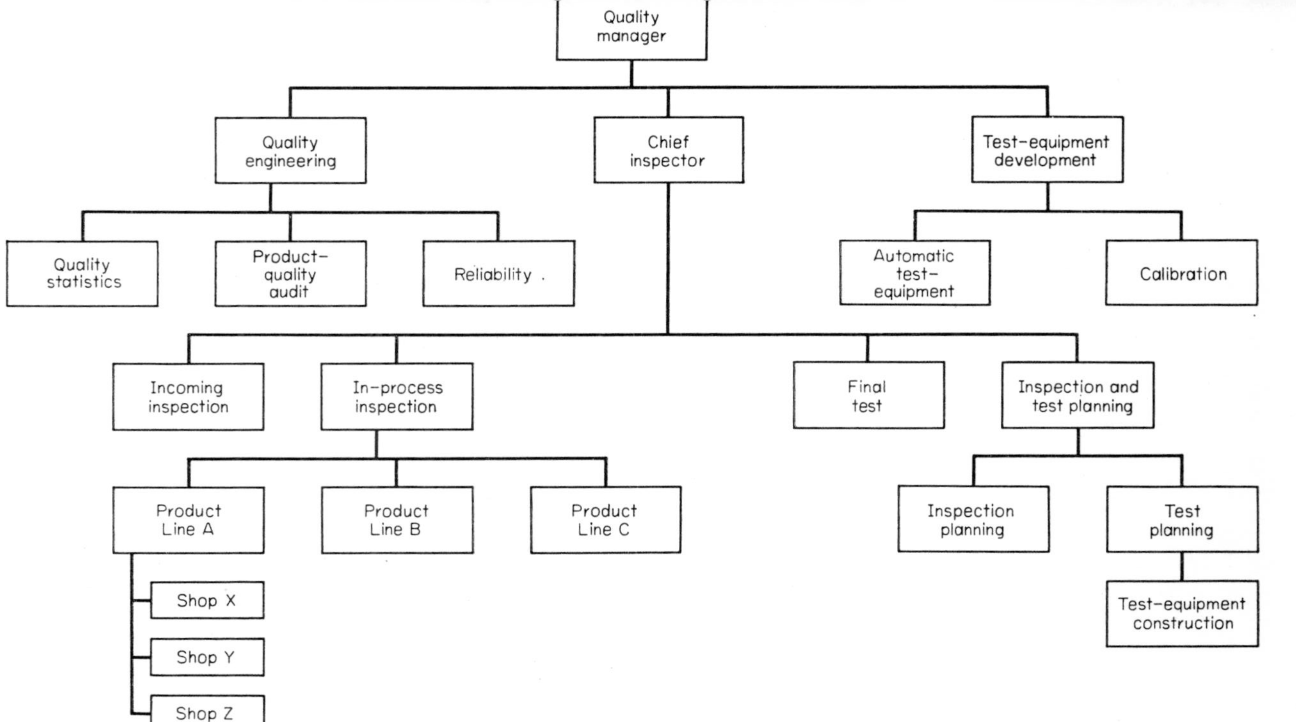

FIGURE 3.2 **Example of an inefficient quality department organization**

rare for good product to spend long periods in final test. If the product is late it is usually the fault of Manufacturing (sometimes Marketing or Engineering). All the general manager has to do is remember that.

"The quality manager spends all of his time chasing product through inspection and test. Transfer inspection and test to production and he can really work on quality." In practice this is more of a problem than the previous one. The answer is to have a good section head in final test and to give the manufacturing manager direct access to him for scheduling. The quality manager should be big enough to do his own job and not need to fill his time being a progress chaser.

"As quality manager, I could stay above the battle and have a nice quiet life if I did not have to run inspection and test." No manager can expect to have a quiet life.

"As quality manager, I am not up to running inspection and test and quality control. If I only had quality control I could cope." A manager is needed who can cope.

"The manufacturing manager must be given all resources needed to make the product." An equally valid position is: the manufacturing manager's job is to see the product is made right the first time.

"Manufacturing must be able to schedule priorities in final test." Agreed—but there is no difficulty in giving this right to Manufacturing even where test reports to Quality.

"In-process inspection and test are an intrinsic part of the manufacturing process." This is true but not relevant to the organizational question.

"If inspection and test report to manufacturing it is easier to redeploy people as the job changes." This is a valid point, but a small one.

"Manufacturing will make inspection and test more efficient by application of work study, automatic test methods, etc." This is usually not true. Most manufacturing people are not especially interested in inspection and test (which are either dull or over-specialized), so these are the last areas where they apply advanced methods. Inspection and test are so important to quality people that they are forced to be interested and advanced methods have been applied more where inspection and test sections report to Quality. Of course, a very good manufacturing manager may achieve more than a below-standard quality manager, but this is the effect of the people, not the organization.

"Make the inspectors and testers fix the defects. This saves all the paperwork and shuffling the product back and forth." It also takes the pressure off doing the job right first time, inhibits efficient inspection and test, and removes an important source of defect-prevention information.

"The testers are adding value by adjusting." This may be a valid point—but what is the major content of the job?

Inspection and test, in practice, bear the major direct responsibility for ensuring that the product conforms to its requirements. This is prejudiced if they report to Manufacturing, whose primary motivator is schedule (cost is second and quality third). Either outgoing quality suffers or an additional "quality audit", reporting to the quality department, is set up, and given responsibility for the outgoing quality. To be able to carry out this responsibility, the audit group needs to be about half the size of the final inspection and test groups and have a duplicate set of expensive test equipment. Of course, this does not happen, so in practice the responsibility for quality assurance is divided and uncertain. However, the "audit" group does get big enough to be very expensive. If inspection and test report to Quality, responsibility for quality assurance can be (and should be) placed definitely on final test and inspection. Duplication is prevented and the quality audit can now be a real audit, carried out by a tiny group for management information only. A good test is: if the quality audit is more than one or two people, money can be saved and quality improved, if management wants it.

Where all inspection and test is done by Quality there is no hiding the "appraisal" costs. The general manager can require the quality manager to carry out planned headcount reductions by improving test and inspection efficiency and, together with Manufacturing and Engineering, by improving the quality of product submitted to test and inspection.

All defect prevention starts with quality data. The cheapest source of this is inspection and test. Where inspection and test report to manufacturing, they will usually not provide good data and a separate, expensive quality data gathering group is established.

Manufacturing, engineering and marketing are big, strong departments. Without inspection and test the quality department is a little, weak department and even where he reports to the general manager, the quality manager is unlikely to be of good calibre. To run inspection, test and quality control adequately is a big job, justifying a first-class man and a good salary. Having inspection and test does not make much difference to the manufacturing department, but it makes a big difference to the quality department. It also improves the balance of the unit as a whole.

Where inspection and test report to Manufacturing, it is easy for the product to be made badly, the defects to be found with an excess of inspection and to be put right with an excess of re-work. All of this happens within the manufacturing department and it need have no clear visibility outside the department. It takes positive resolution on the part of manufacturing management to prevent it, and often resolution is lacking.

THE ORGANIZATIONAL POSITION OF THE QUALITY DEPARTMENT

In the last section it was noted that there were two particularly controversial points with regard to the organization of the quality department. The first, which was dealt with in that section, was whether inspection and test should be part of the manufacturing or quality department. The second concerns the position of the quality department in the organization of the unit as a whole. It is very common to find even a strong, integrated quality department reporting to the manufacturing manager with the quality manager at the same reporting level as the production superintendent, the chief industrial engineer, the production-control manager, etc.

This is wrong. For a number of reasons the quality department should report at the same level as the manufacturing department, the engineering department, and the marketing department. This means that the quality manager should report to the general manager. The first reason for this is that the quality department has the final responsibility for ensuring that only product that conforms to its requirement is sent to the customer. It cannot consistently meet this responsibility when the quality manager reports to the manufacturing manager. Even where the manufacturing manager is of high integrity and well aware of his quality responsibilities, and never directly overrules his quality manager, the pressures of meeting schedule are subtly communicated to the quality manager, and can erode his fulfilment of his quality responsibilities.

The second reason is possibly more important. While Quality remains effectively a section of the manufacturing department it is most unlikely to have effective relationships with the engineering, marketing and accounting departments. It was noted above that the quality department should audit the quality-relevant activities of these departments (and Manufacturing) and report to the department managers and the general manager. This is clearly a very difficult task that will only be carried out under the leadership of a strong quality manager and with the support of the general manager: it is quite unrealistic to expect a section of the manufacturing department to perform it satisfactorily.

The most serious product problems have their genesis in the marketing-development phase of new-product introduction. Quality techniques that can assist in the avoidance of these problems will be described in Chapter 8, but the quality department can only play its part in these if it can meet the engineering and marketing departments on terms of equality.

The need for the quality department to be independent of the manufacturing and engineering departments is not a reflection of the "importance" of the quality department. The quality responsibilities of the company as a whole cannot be over-emphasized, but the quality department as such bears only a part of those responsibilities. It can be argued that the quality department is not as important as the manufacturing department or the engineering department, so why should it report at the same level? Equal claims for importance can be made for the purchasing section or production control and these are part of Manufacturing. The quality department has to be independent in order to do its job, and views about its importance compared to other groups within the company are largely irrelevant to this point.

STAFF QUALITY DIRECTORS, QUALITY MANAGERS AND QUALITY COUNCILS

In the last two sections the implicit assumption has been made that we have been concerned with a separate unit, led by a general manager and concerned with the development, manufacture and sales of a restricted range of products. It has been argued that such a unit should have a separate quality department reporting to the general manager. However, much of modern industry is organized within vast companies making a diverse range of products, in innumerable factories and plants at widely spaced geographic locations, and, in the case of the international conglomerates, in many different countries.

The organization of the quality function within such a company will obviously be dependent upon its overall organization, but some general principles can be established. Very often the company will contain some separate units, led by general managers with profit responsibility. In this case the quality organization within each unit can be as described above. However, the large company has the opportunity to increase the overall efficiency of the quality function by integrating, to some extent, the activity across the company as a whole. All too often this opportunity is missed and the quality departments of the units work in isolation from each other. This is particularly so where Quality is merely a section within the manufacturing department. The manufacturing managers of the units may get together (though for some reason they seem to do this less than technical managers and chief accountants) and they may also have their activities guided by a manufacturing director, but this does not extend down into the quality sections.

Figure 3.3 illustrates, in simplified form, the kind of organization that can be used to integrate quality activities across a large multi-unit company. The situation in a real company will usually be more complex than that illustrated in the figure with several separate units, not just two, more functions than technical, marketing, manufacturing and quality, and interrelationships between functional directors and the unit functional managers. For the quality function the line quality managers in the units report directly to their unit general managers but they also have a functional responsibility to the quality director.

The quality director has a staff position and, unlike the line quality managers, who may lead departments of several hundred people, he may work alone or with a few senior quality engineers. The task of the quality director is to give leadership to the quality function throughout the company as a whole. He will be concerned with persuading the unit general managers to reorganize their quality departments in a more effective manner, in establishing the company policies for quality, in giving assistance to units with special problems, in carrying out independent quality audits and in co-operating with the other headquarters staff groups, for engineering, manufacturing, etc. A major responsibility is in training and motivating the unit quality departments to extend their activities beyond inspection and test into the full range of quality techniques appropriate to their circumstances. The quality director is, of course, responsible for reporting the overall quality status of the company to the company's top management.

One frequent complicating situation in a real company is for the products of a unit to be manufactured at one or more plants which are geographically separate from the unit headquarters, where marketing and new-product development take place. In this situation it may not be practical to have a comprehensive unit quality department with all inspection, test and quality staff reporting directly to a central unit quality manager. It can then be acceptable to have plant quality managers who report directly to the plant managers and have a functional responsibility either to the unit quality manager or directly to the company quality director. In these circumstances it is probable that the plant quality department will be ineffective in performing the quality activities relevant to Engineering and Marketing, for example design review and qualification-testing, and it may be best to transfer responsibility for these activities, and also perhaps for product and system audits, to a central quality group at the unit or company level. The transfer of functions in this way necessarily means that the numbers of people in the central group must be increased beyond that which would be adequate for a purely staff responsibility.

An extremely important method of improving the efficiency and

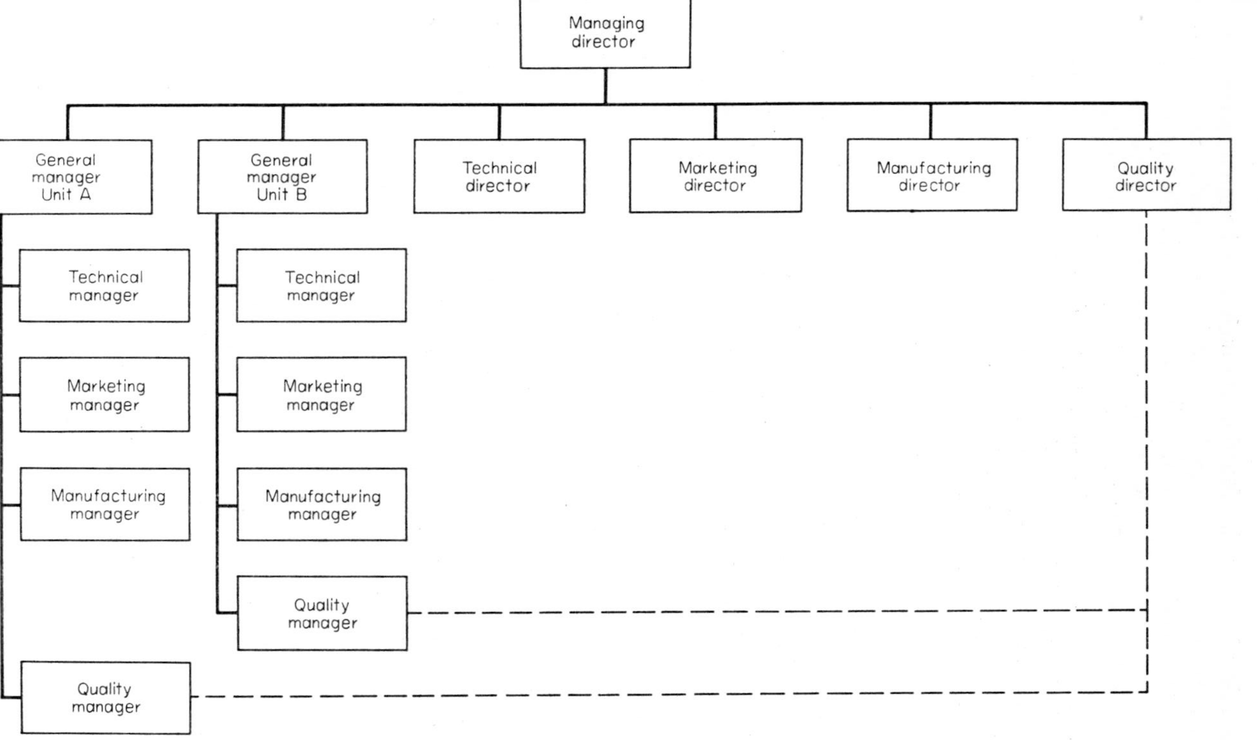

FIGURE 3.3 **Quality organization within a multi-unit company**

morale of the quality function throughout a large company is to establish one or more quality councils. The quality manager of every unit should be a member of such a council. The purpose of the councils is to enable the unit quality departments to co-operate in developing and applying methods of improving their effectiveness. They can be used by the central company quality staff as a means of introducing company policies, and in this case the principles of how the policies can be applied in the units can be developed within the councils. Equally, the councils can themselves highlight a need—for example, the need for co-operation in source inspection at vendors—and then develop the methods to satisfy the need.

Of the three methods of improving the effectiveness of quality departments (each unit to develop its own improvements in isolation; improvements to be devised by central staff groups and imposed on the units; units to co-operate in developing improvements through councils), the best is undoubtedly a fruitful interaction betweeen an efficient central staff and active and enthusiastic councils.

Many of the largest companies in the world have not attempted to establish a policy on quality for the company as a whole. They have no vice-president or director at the company level, and are content to consider quality as a matter for the individual units (or sub-units) from which they are composed. In this they miss a great opportunity. Some of the units may do well, most will be mediocre and a few will have disasters. International Telephones and Telegraphs is perhaps the most complex company of all. With sales in 1970 of over 5,000 million dollars it is the ninth largest company in the world. It is completely international, operating in over fifty different countries (the units whose activities are co-ordinated through ITT Europe alone have sales of 2,000 million dollars) and has a range of activities which has extended from its traditional base in telecommunications into car hire, hotels, food industry, insurance and many others. This vast company has an overall quality policy and quality is a major preoccupation of its top managers. Under the leadership of its Director–Quality, Vice-President P. B. Crosby, this policy has been implemented—not perfectly but with major impact—across the whole company. The chief tools for this company-wide activity have been the central staff groups in New York and the area headquarters, e.g. Brussels for Europe—in all, less than ten people—the staff people in the unit headquarters, and the line quality managers, all communicating and interacting through a world-wide system of quality councils.

For ITT (Europe) there are five regional quality councils, the first embracing Germany, Austria and Switzerland, the second Spain and Portugal and so on. Grouping is largely by language to ease communication. Membership of each of these regional councils consists of ten or twelve of the senior quality managers of the ITT companies in the region. Sub-councils, reporting to the regional councils, then cover all the more junior quality managers. The regional councils meet four to six times each year. In addition to the regional councils, there are product councils, involving the quality managers from ITT (Europe) as a whole who are in units concerned with particular products or activities, e.g. electronic components, consumer products, electronic telephone exchanges, installation, etc. These councils also meet regularly in different locations throughout Europe and the members together develop and apply the systems they need to control their products.

The chairmen of the regional councils and the product councils in the main form the membership of the European executive quality council, the most senior council in ITT (Europe), to which all of the other councils report. This council meets three times a year and is responsible for establishing and guiding the activities of the other councils. ITT has similar council systems in other areas of the world, e.g. North America and Latin America, and the European executive quality council meets with its opposite members from these other areas every one to two years, as the ITT World-wide Council.

The whole council system operates independently of outside direction. It appoints its own chairmen and secretaries, draws up its own programmes of work and organizes its own meetings. There is, of course, a continuing and fruitful interaction with the senior quality staff from the world and area headquarters. The council system also gives Quality a means of working effectively with other functions, Technical, Accounting, Installation, etc., on overall company programmes of standardization and co-ordination.

The organization of the ITT system of quality councils has been described in some detail because it has proved a successful means of upgrading the effectiveness of quality departments throughout a vast company, and it may give a model usable by other companies. Without some such system it is difficult to see how an overall company policy of quality improvement could be implemented. The price to be paid, of allowing quality managers to be absent from their plants for one or two days a few times a year, is a small one.

4 The Quality-Improvement Programme

In Chapter 1 it was stated that a business had two quality objectives, which were:

(i) to supply products to customers that conform to their requirements;

(ii) to minimize quality costs.

The management of a company may decide that it wishes to make a major improvement in the level of achievement of these objectives. This decision may arise for a number of reasons. The complaints of product non-conformance from major customers may have become insistent and a serious effect on product sales may be resulting. The level of product rejection by inspection and test and consequent re-work may be causing serious disorganization of production so that delivery schedules are missed, costs are inflated and inventory is out of control. These are negative reasons for action. More positively, earlier decisions may have caused the establishment of an effective quality department, and consequent reports of quality-cost and product-conformance levels may have shown management that important additions to profits could result from improvement in the quality area. In a large company, the management of a particular unit may have been influenced by an overall company policy proselytized by central quality staff and reinforced through a quality-council system (see Chapter 3).

Having made the decision to improve, for whatever reason, the unit management is then faced with the problem of how to do it. There is only one effective solution to this problem: for the general manager to lead and participate in a planned quality-improvement programme involving the unit as a whole. Limitation of the programme to particular areas, e.g. the quality department, and absence of management participation will ensure that the programme will be ineffective.

The concept of quality improvement was formalized by P. B. Crosby at the Martin Company in the USA in 1961 and has been further developed by many companies since then.[1] As used in ITT, the quality-improvement programme is a 14-step procedure aimed at defect prevention and summarized in a short booklet entitled *Quality Improvement through Defect Prevention.* Of course, many variations of the programme are possible and many of its elements reflect long-established quality-control principles. But the need for an overall planned programme is inescapable and, in practice, although there have been many attempts, it has not proved possible to devise effective procedures that have departed seriously from the steps given in the quality-improvement booklet.

Although originated in the USA, the programme has now been applied with striking success in many European countries. In the UK one unit was receiving serious complaints about product conformance from its major customer. By applying the programme, for nine major product lines the percentage defective as recorded by the customer was reduced by a factor of 4. At the same time the ratio of testers and inspectors to direct operatives was reduced by 21 per cent. In Germany another unit reduced its quality-cost to sales ratio in 1968 to 86·4 per cent of the 1967 value and in 1969 to 80·2 per cent, thereby saving DM 3·4 million. Various measures of level of conformance improved simultaneously: tool-making defects were reduced from 4·0 per cent to 1·2 per cent; defective pieceparts were reduced from 3·2 per cent to 0·4 per cent; electronic assembly defects on printed circuit boards were reduced to one-eighth and so on. During six months the average number of defects made by each worker was reduced from forty per month to ten per month. In Italy a company reduced its quality-cost to sales ratio from 9·0 per cent in 1968 to 7·5 per cent in 1969 and 7·4 per cent in 1970. In Belgium another company reduced the ratio from 8·8 per cent in 1969 to 7·5 per cent in 1970, saving BF 95 million. Both these companies improved their level of product conformance simultaneously. Other examples could be given involving companies in Spain, Portugal and France. In all cases quality costs were reduced but with no sacrifice of quality—in fact there was an improvement in the level of product conformance.

[1] See Philip B. Crosby, *Cutting the Cost of Quality* (Industrial Education Institute, 1947).

MANAGEMENT COMMITMENT

The fourteen steps of the quality improvement programme are summarized in Figure 4.1, which also gives a time-table for their application extending over one year.

The first step is "management commitment". Without an active commitment by the general manager of the unit and full support by all of his department heads the major benefits of the programme cannot be achieved. In all the successful programmes described above the complete support of the unit general manager was a common feature.

In addition to the commitment of active support for the whole quality-improvement programme, the general manager at the start of the programme should formally state the quality policy of the unit and publicize it so that everyone in the unit is completely familiar with it. The ITT quality-improvement booklet lists five things that the quality policy should not be:

"1. It should not be a treatise on the 'Economics of Quality'. There is no such thing as an Economical Level of Quality and it is always cheaper to do the job properly. There are economic levels of inspection, test laboratory equipment, secretaries, food servings and other functions, but there is no 'Economic Level of Quality'."

"2. The Quality Policy should not have a number in it. Stating allowable non-conformance is no way to get what you want because no one notices the number for what it is. They just know it is there and allow for it."

"3. It should not indicate any method of deviating from the policy. If it does immediately there will be a procedure written on that method and meetings will be held to train people extensively in the procedure—to the reduction of the original intent."

"4. It should not delegate the responsibility for evaluating performance to the policy. This must be the prerogative of the Chief Executive even though he will have others gather the information for him."

"5. The policy should not be hidden in a book reserved for executive personnel only. It should be stated, re-stated and publicized until everyone knows, understands and believes it."

In Chapter 1 the quality policy used by ITT was given: "Perform exactly like the Requirement . . . or cause the Requirement to be officially changed to what we and our customers really need."

Different words may be used for stating the policy of a unit, but a quality-improvement programme must start from a commitment by the unit's manager to make and supply products that conform exactly to requirements. Once that commitment is made the energies of all

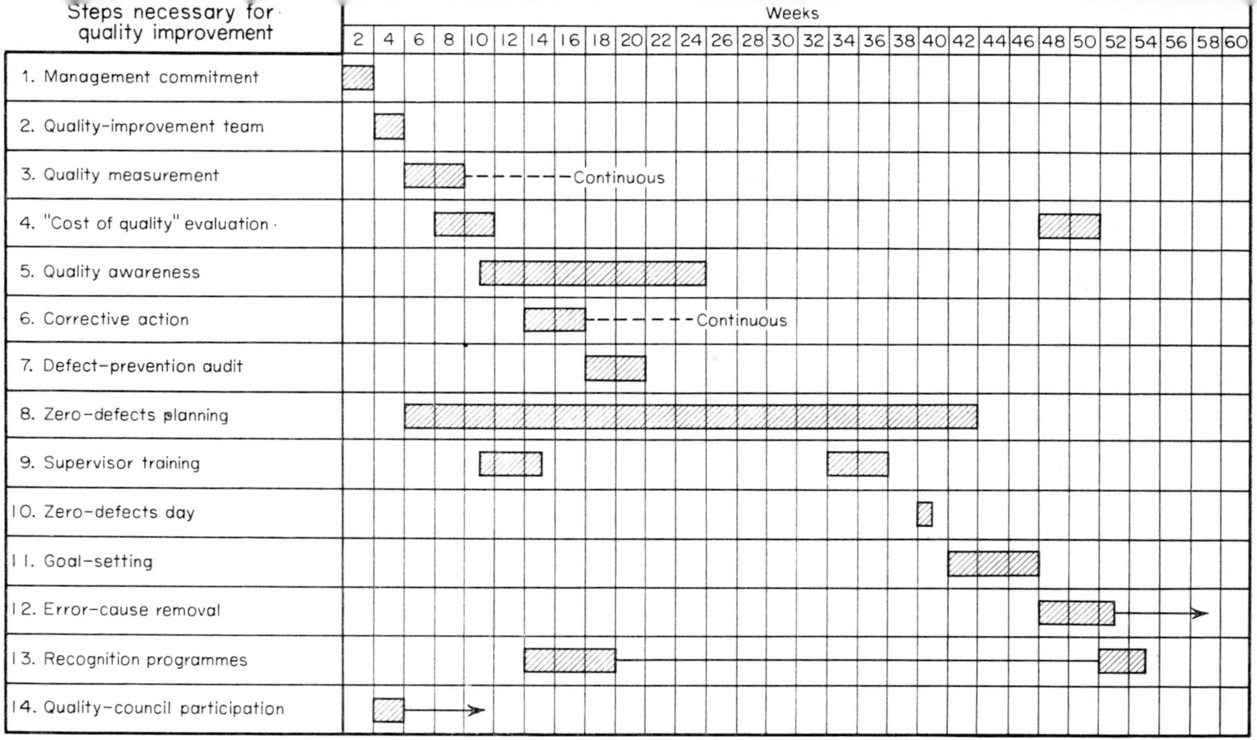

Steps necessary for quality improvement	Weeks
	2 4 6 8 10 12 14 16 18 20 22 24 26 28 30 32 34 36 38 40 42 44 46 48 50 52 54 56 58 60
1. Management commitment	
2. Quality-improvement team	
3. Quality measurement	Continuous
4. "Cost of quality" evaluation	
5. Quality awareness	
6. Corrective action	Continuous
7. Defect-prevention audit	
8. Zero-defects planning	
9. Supervisor training	
10. Zero-defects day	
11. Goal-setting	
12. Error-cause removal	
13. Recognition programmes	
14. Quality-council participation	

FIGURE 4.1 **Time schedule**

the personnel of the unit can be directed at determining how this can be done most easily and cheaply. In its absence much effort is wasted by individual groups within the unit determining how much they can "get away with" and by different groups coping with defective material received from other groups.

The second part of the policy is as important as the first. When no one really expects to conform exactly to the requirement it is not very important that the requirement is not precisely defined. A commitment to exact conformance changes completely the status of the requirement. This applies not only to the final product going to the customer, but also to all of the items from which it is made. A frequent early consequence of the start of a quality-improvement programme is an energetic revaluation of specifications and particularly of the tolerances of dimensions on pieceparts. The design department, having no confidence in the machine shop's will to make conforming parts, includes a safety factor on the specified tolerances making them tighter than necessary. The machine shop, of course, knows this and has a strong disincentive to exact conformance. The result is confusion. The way out of the confusion is for the quality department to determine and report which of the parts are non-conformant. The Pareto principle is applied, i. e. the most important parts are examined first. Manufacturing engineering and Production then determine how to improve to meet the tolerances really required and the design department relaxes those tolerances that are tighter than needed.

There is one other key aspect of the management commitment step of the quality-improvement programme. This is for the general manager to establish the quality-improvement team.

THE QUALITY-IMPROVEMENT TEAM

The quality-improvement programme involves the unit as a whole, and every department has its contribution to make. Many of these contributions are simply performing correctly those normal responsibilities of the department which relate to product quality. One of the principal ways in which the quality-improvement programme achieves its effect is in highlighting these activities, defining schedules for improvement and monitoring their achievement. The quality-improvement team is the means for doing this.

The overall purpose of the team is to provide guidance for the quality-improvement programme. It consists of senior members of each of the departments involved in the programme working on a part-time basis. It is led by a chairman appointed by the general manager. For the chairman the quality-improvement programme will be a major activity and he will obviously have a key effect on the success or failure of the whole programme. He must satisfy two main requirements: he must be a mature member of the unit's management team, in whom the general manager and his department heads have confidence and he must fully understand the objectives and methods of the quality-improvement programme and have wholehearted agreement with them. It is not necessary that he should be a member of the quality department: managers from manufacturing, personnel, engineering and other departments have led quality-improvement programmes with success.

As given in the quality-improvement booklet the responsibilities of the members of the team are to:

"1. Lay out the entire quality-improvement programme;
2. Represent their department on the team;
3. Cause the decisions of the team to be executed in their department;
4. Contribute creatively to the implementation of the improvement activity."

The team should develop a plan for the implementation of the whole programme within the unit and should define the dates at which each of the steps will be accomplished. The plan should be presented to the general manager and his department heads for approval and support. The general manager should also attend some of the meetings of the team, not only at the beginning, but as the programme continues. The examples of its application given earlier in this chapter make it clear that a successful quality-improvement programme is not completed in a few weeks. It is a continuing activity extending over a long period and it will only be maintained at an effective level if the general manager attends some of the meetings of the quality-improvement team. He should also require regular reporting of the results of the programme at his staff meeting and ensure completion of agreed actions.

The specific responsibilities of the team with regard to the programme as a whole will be dealt with below under the various steps of the programme.

Quality Measurement and Quality-cost Reporting

If the energies and enthusiasm released by the management commitment to quality improvement and by the establishment of the interfunctional quality-improvement team are to be effective, it is necessary for them to be directed at solution of the most important problems. This is only possible if quality measurement and quality-cost reporting systems are working. Quality-cost reporting has been discussed in detail in Chapter 2. One of the principal reasons for setting up a quality-cost reporting system is to give management a means of identifying the improvement actions that will produce the biggest effects. Is re-work the major problem, or electrical test? Are warranty costs high? Is the main problem with product line A, or is product line B the one requiring early attention? Quality-cost reporting enables these questions to be answered. It also gives one very important and clear method of establishing targets for improvement and enables management to know whether improvement actions are being effective. Quality-cost reporting is an important responsibility of the comptroller's department.

Of equal importance is quality measurement. By quality measurement is meant the measurement of the level of conformance of the product to its requirements through the various stages of manufacture from incoming parts to the final product sold to the customer or installed on his premises. Quality measurement is a direct responsibility of the quality department and it is almost never done well except by an efficient quality department.

Quality control has been traditionally concerned with the systematic accumulation of quantitative data on products and processes and the statistical analysis of these data for control purposes. Quality measurement in the context of a quality-improvement programme gives a different emphasis to this activity. The aim is to provide very simple information that can be immediately understood by people outside the quality department. These may be purchasing buyers, industrial engineers, production supervisors, managers at all levels, and the shop-floor operators themselves. The purpose of quality measurement is to help these people to improve—by providing quality data that they can understand with little effort and without explanation from specialist staff.

A few examples of such information and the methods by which it can be presented will now be given. After a component or sub-assembly is made it is usually inspected or tested. Very often this is a 100 per cent operation having the principal purpose of enabling defective items to be screened out, for scrap or re-work. However, if the inspectors are required to fill in simple defect sheets the inspection can additionally provide quality-measurement data. This can then be graphed on a chart of percentage defective against time. Quality-measurement information can also be obtained from the results of acceptance-sampling inspections and product-quality audits (see Chapter 6). Figure 4.2 gives an example of such a chart for electrical relays used in the assembly of equipment for telephone exchanges. These relays are manually adjusted after assembly and the various gaps and tensions are checked by inspection. Defective relays are then readjusted. A large chart such as that illustrated in Figure 4.2 can be mounted in the relay-adjustment shop. Smaller charts can be completed by the inspectors for each adjustment operator. These can be given to the production supervisor for the shop or preferably can be mounted against each operator. Quality-measurement information af this kind is immediately understandable by the production supervisor and by the operators. It gives them a measure of performance, comparison of individual operators, and lets them know whether they are improving or deteriorating.

An alternative approach is to put the emphasis not upon the proportion of items that are defective but upon the number of defects actually made. These can then be graphed as defects per 100 items (where the item is simple) or as defects per item for a complex item. Figure 4.3 gives an example of the former for printed-board assemblies, which are a major sub-assembly of modern electronic equipment. They consist of flat plates made of insulating material through which a pattern of holes is punched or drilled. These holes are connected by an arrangement of copper tracks plated on to the surface of the insulating plate. The leads of electronic components are inserted through the holes. The printed boards are then passed through a machine which solders the component leads to the copper tracks. In this way the components are connected together without using wiring. Usually however a proportion of the component leads will not solder properly. These defects must be found by visually inspecting the printed-board assemblies and they are then "touched-up" manually using a soldering iron. One way of measuring the success of the machine-soldering process would be to measure the proportion of board assemblies which was defective. However these assemblies differ widely in complexity. Some may contain only twenty or thirty solder joints whereas others may contain several hundred. It is obviously much more likely for boards of the latter type to be defective (i.e. contain at least one defective joint) than the former. A better measure therefore is defects per 100 solder joints, as given in Figure 4.3.

A graph of this kind shows very clearly whether the process is in trouble and then if actions taken to improve have been effective. Another kind of simple analysis is often used as a means of indicating the kind of action needed. This is to determine the relative frequency of different kinds of defects. In Figure 4.4 this type of analysis has been applied to the set of results plotted in Figure 4.3. It shows that the major defect categories are spikes of solder and non-wetting of the component leads. The actions to be taken to prevent defects of this kind in future soldering are likely to be different from those that would have been taken if there had been more joints with holes or more "button" joints.

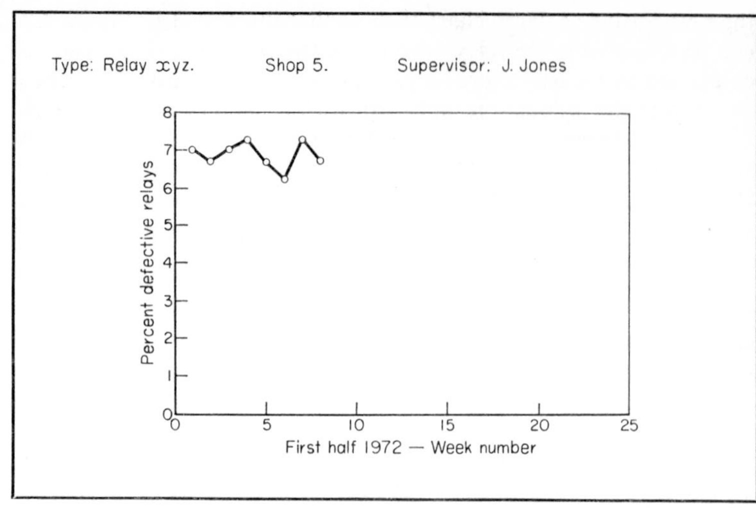

FIGURE 4.2 **Graph of percentage defective for telephone-exchange relays**

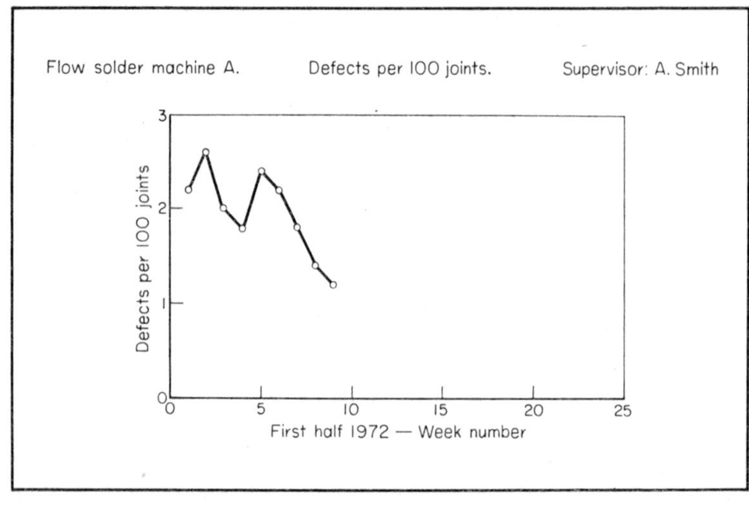

FIGURE 4.3 **Graph of defects per 100 solder joints on printed-board assemblies**

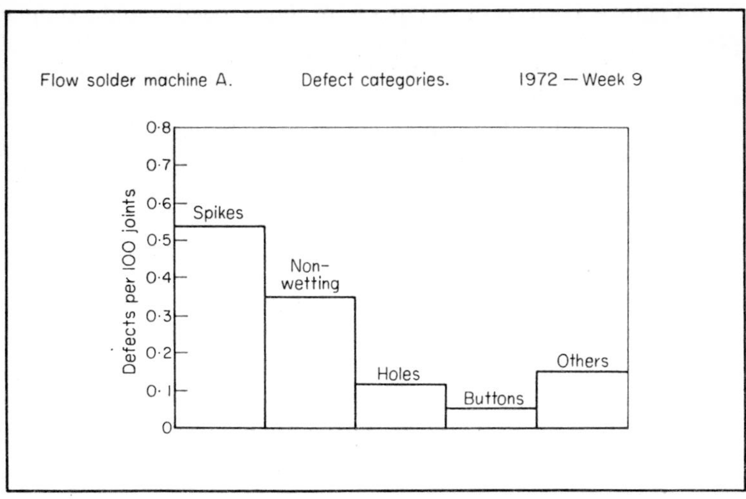

FIGURE 4.4 **Chart of relative frequency of different kinds of solder-joint defects**

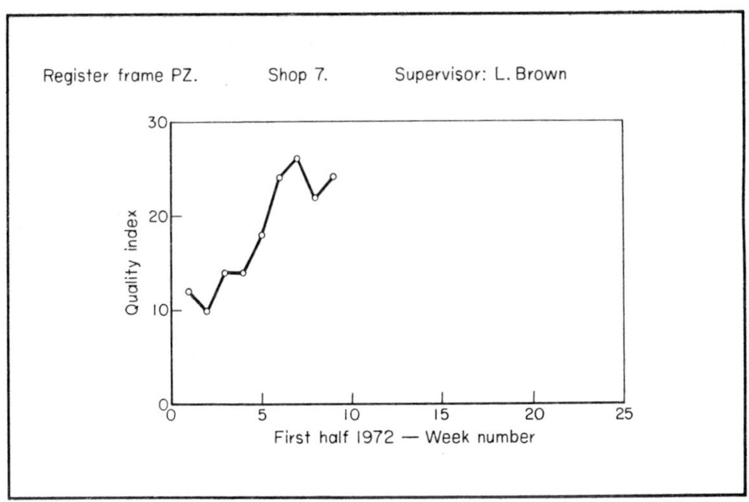

FIGURE 4.5 **Chart of quality index for a complex sub-assembly**

In Figure 4.3 defects of all types were added together and a simple graph plotted of defects per 100 joints against week number. In some cases it is useful to categorize the defects as major or minor and plot two lines on the graph. For example, it might be true that non-wetted joints and button joints were much more likely to give open circuits and therefore cause failure of the ultimate equipment during use, than spikes or holes. The latter would be categorized as minor defects and a small proportion might be tolerable in the ultimate equipment. All button joints and non-wetted joints found at this stage would be classed as major defects and require re-work. Even this additional complexity should be avoided if possible. The aim is to communicate effectively with the various people who may have to take corrective action. The more complicated the means of communication the greater the likelihood that some or all of these people will be unable to understand, or, more likely, will not be prepared to take the trouble to understand.

Many mechanical, electrical and electronic assemblies and sub-assemblies have many tens or even hundreds of possible defect types, which vary in importance from small imperfections in, say, paint finish to defects requiring the whole unit to be scrapped. One method of dealing with this situation is to give each defect type a weighting between 1 and 10 or 1 and 100 depending upon its importance. (The method of weighting is usually mainly subjective.) The numbers of defects of each type found on a unit are multiplied by the appropriate weightings and all of the resulting numbers added together to give a "quality index". The quality index can then be plotted week by week as in Figure 4.5. Charts of this kind are of little or no use. They are not understood by the people who must take action to prevent defects. For example, Figure 4.5 produces no reaction other than puzzlement in the reader. Is the product in a good state or a bad state? If the latter, where must corrective action be concentrated? Is the situation improving or deteriorating? The chart does not give an answer to these questions. Of course, the chart could be made more explicit by adding information, but then the complexity is increased. Compare Figure 4.5 with Figures 4.2 and 4.3. The reader may have no formal knowledge of relays but Figure 4.2 will suggest to him that the relay quality is neither improving nor deteriorating, it is probably not very good and could fairly easily be improved, but it is not at a crisis level. Figures 4.3 and 4.4 together give an even clearer picture of the state of the particular flow-soldering operation being measured.

All charts should be self-explanatory. Few people will remember required back-up information and virtually none will take the trouble to refer to filed explanations. Quality indices are often only understood by the person who prepares them. Where the defect situation is complex one answer is to ignore the trivial defects and divide the others into major and minor categories. Or it may be necessary to use several simple, self-explanatory graphs. It is quicker to look at three or four charts, each one of which is immediately understood, than to puzzle over one which is not.

One technique which can be used to relate the quality performance of operators who are performing a wide variety of different tasks is to measure the number of defects each one produces in a certain time (this can either be actual time, or standard time). An operator who makes only two or three defects in a week's work is unlikely to have any major problems. One who produces forty or fifty almost certainly has. The operator may be bad or the task may be too difficult, but either way action is required.

The examples given of methods of quality measurement have been very simple, because these are the methods that are most effective in assisting defect prevention. Nothing has been included about statistical techniques which are often applied to such measurements. For example, the percentage defective chart of Figure 4.2 is called a "p" chart in statistical quality-control jargon and "control" limits can be applied to such a chart. Although the mathematics needed to determine control limits is quite simple, it needs the time of a quality engineer to set up the method and a quality technician to apply it. And then the people using the chart will not understand control limits at all if they have not been to special training courses and only imperfectly if they have. To use a p or a similar chart with statistical correctness is very important when the purpose is to control some process as precisely as possible, to take action quickly when the data indicate the need, and to refrain from action until the data show that the process has actually changed. Quality-measurement charts in the context of a quality-improvement programme are often used to show the defect level in a static situation and improvement trends can usually be established over a relatively long period. It is not therefore necessary to know the statistical significance of individual points on the chart. This means that the number of quality-measurement charts is not limited by the availability of quality engineers expert in statistical quality control.

The essence of the quality-improvement programme is that all functions of the unit are involved and that most defect prevention work and corrective actions will come, not from the quality department, but from other departments, production, purchasing, engineering, industrial engineering, etc. These are the people for whom the quality-measurement information is intended—and for the general manager, whose interest will have a major effect on the success or otherwise of the programme. Quality-measurement information must be out in the open, widely displayed, simple and understood by everyone. It must not be a secret method by which one quality engineer communicates with another.

Quality Awareness

The fifth and sixth steps of the quality-improvement programme are called "quality awareness" and "corrective action". The purpose of the former is to increase the consciousness of quality and product conformance of everyone in the unit. At this stage the methods used should be fairly unobtrusive. Posters with a quality theme should be mounted in the production shops, laboratories and offices, and articles dealing with quality should be published in the house magazine. In addition quality and defect prevention should become an active discussion point at meetings between workers and supervisors and management.

The cost of the quality-awareness step can be quite small. Some companies run quality poster competitions for their employees and their families. Small prizes are given to the winners and a whole series of posters is obtained.

The quality-awareness step is organized by the quality-improvement team using the specialist help of the public relations and industrial relations departments.

Corrective Action

The corrective-action step of the programme is obviously of great importance. A major purpose of the earlier steps is to provide conditions under which corrective actions can be made effectively. The management commitment, the establishment of the inter-departmental quality-improvement team and the quality-awareness campaign should give the necessary personal involvement for action. The quality-cost reporting and quality-measurement data should determine where improvement is most needed and enable progress to be followed.

The purposes of corrective action are first to enable defective product to be brought into conformance. This may be no more than an extension of re-work to cover situations in which the re-work methods to be used are not obvious. The second purpose is more important. This is to solve problems giving rise to non-conformant product in such a manner that defects are prevented in the future—and to do this in such a way that each problem is solved once and for all. Particular attention is given to chronic problems, which the system has learnt to adjust to, but which cause excessive screening, scrap and re-work and which allow a proportion of non-conformant product to reach the customer.

An inadequate level of effective corrective action is not usually a result of insufficient technical knowledge about how to solve the problems. The necessary expertise is usually available within the unit. The reason is that there is no organizational framework for presenting each problem to the particular group able to solve it. And there is an absence of management policy that all groups shall give a high priority to the solution of product non-conformance and quality-cost problems.

The organizational framework is provided by defining responsibility at a number of levels. First, in each manufacturing area there should be a short meeting every day between the production supervisor and the appropriate representative of the quality department. Problems detected should be examined and methods of correcting them should be determined, the emphasis being upon permanent solutions. It is important that these actions should be documented in a simple chart (see Figure 4.6) as a means of giving discipline to the activity. The chart should list each problem, who has accepted responsibility for its solution, the proposed action and the date scheduled for completion of the action. These charts should be maintained by each quality department representative and should be reviewed by the quality manager or his delegate to ensure that they are completed conscientiously.

At the next level production general supervision should meet each week with senior quality management to attack problems that could not be solved at the lower level. Many problems will involve action from other departments, purchasing, training, design engineering, etc. These departments will be called upon as required by the individual shop activity described in the last paragraph and representatives should be invited to attend the weekly meetings. Again it is important that quality engineering should document the weekly meetings in the same kind of action chart as that described above.

At the highest level the general manager and his staff should review unresolved problems at monthly or special meetings, It is only in this way that the priority status of the whole corrective-action programme can be maintained. Solution of some problems will require allocation of resources that can only be made at the general-manager level. Others may have a level of technical difficulty that will require establishment of particular task teams, to work over a relatively long period. Quality management is responsible for ensuring that all problems presented at this level are defined in a specific manner.

An effective corrective-action system will give a major reduction of quality costs and will improve the level of product conformance. It

Number	Date	Problem	Action	Responsible	Completion	
					Scheduled	Achieved
28	14.3.72	Weak thermo compression bonds	Re-train two operators	C. Brown	28.3.72	
29	18.3.72	Non-hermetic seals	Screen defective lot by helium Reset welder	C. Brown V. White	19.3.72 18.3.72	19.3.72 18.3.72

FIGURE 4.6 **Corrective-action log**

will also simplify production control by eliminating or reducing re-work cycles, simplify scheduling and reduce work-in-process inventory.

DEFECT-PREVENTION AUDIT

One method of defect prevention is to analyse the defects that are present in current product, place them in a priority list of importance and take corrective action, so that similar defects are not produced in future product. The earlier steps of the programme, particularly the quality-cost and quality-measuring steps and the corrective-action step, utilize this method. Another approach is to examine the overall operating *system* with respect to its ability to prevent defects, and to take action to improve the system on the basis of the situation found. Such an examination is called a defect-prevention audit. It is analogous to the audits carried out of suppliers to determine their capability of supplying product conforming to specification. However, within the unit itself the audit can be carried out more exhaustively. The audit can be performed by the unit quality manager himself or, in a large company, by the company quality director or a member of his staff.

In ITT such audits are carried out against a quality-programme specification which defines the essential elements of the quality system. Table 4.1 gives a list of such elements, covering the general management policy towards the quality function within the unit, the direct activities of the quality department and the activities of other departments which particularly affect product quality.

Each element of the quality system should then be audited. One method of doing this is to prepare a series of questions for each element. Questionnaires of this type have been published for the use of external auditors of companies working on defence contracts requiring compliance with such quality-system specifications as MIL-Q-9858 A in the USA and AVP 92 in the UK. The author and E. W. Karlin of ITT headquarters, New York, have developed rating sheets including a series of questions for each one of the quality-system elements given in Table 4.1. For each question a marking between 0 and 100 is given and the average rating for the element is then determined. Figure 4.7 gives an example of such a rating sheet for one of the direct quality-department activities and shows the method of filling it in. The average rating for this example is 54 per cent. The questions for one of the activities which concern more than one department are given in Table 4.2 on page 64.

TABLE 4.1

Elements of the Quality System

1 *Management quality policy*

2 *Quality-department activities*
- 2.1 Inspection and test
  - 2.1.1 Purchased goods
  - 2.1.2 Fabrication (machine shop, etc.)
  - 2.1.3 Assembly
  - 2.1.4 Final
  - 2.1.5 Shipping
  - 2.1.6 Installation
- 2.2 Quality engineering
  - 2.2.1 Inspection and test planning
  - 2.2.2 Procurement of inspection and test equipment
  - 2.2.3 Quality measurement, analysis and reporting
  - 2.2.4 Quality manual
  - 2.2.5 Participation in unit and other department quality programmes
- 2.3 Supplier quality control
- 2.4 Quality audits
  - 2.4.1 Quality-programme audits
  - 2.4.2 Product audits
  - 2.4.3 Process audits
- 2.5 Quality-council activities

3 *Activities monitored by the quality department*
- 3.1 New-product requirement specification
- 3.2 Customer contract and specification review
- 3.3 Configuration, specification and drawing control
- 3.4 Design review
- 3.5 Process qualification
- 3.6 Product qualification and re-qualification
- 3.7 Test equipment and gauge control
- 3.8 Handling, storage and transportation
- 3.9 Quality-cost reporting
- 3.10 Operator and inspector training and certification
- 3.11 Corrective action
- 3.12 Quality-improvement programme

The auditor completes each one of the rating sheets by discussing the questions with the relevant managers in the quality, engineering, purchasing and other departments. Obviously, the discussion frequently extends beyond the area specifically covered by the questions and there is often an important extension of understanding of quality matters in other department managers as a consequence.

As each succeeding element of the system is audited, an overall "profile" of the effectiveness of the system is built up. For some

Quality-system audit	Unit: XYZ Location: Paris	Auditor: C. Braun Date: 23-7-72 p 13 of 51
Item	**Rating** (0 — 50 — 100)	**Comments**
2.2.3. QUALITY-MEASUREMENT ANALYSIS & REPORTING		
1. Are adequate numbers of trained and supervised technicians and clerks available to analyse and report quality data?		1 technician 2 clerks
2. Are the results of all inspections, tests and product audits recorded in a manner suitable for analysis?		Yes, in assembly and final test. No, in machine shop
3. Is the analysis such that the quality performance of individual operators, processes and equipment is clear?		Only in assembly
4. Are the results of all individual operators and groups of operators published to them in a clear manner to assist defect prevention?		Only in assembly
⁄5. Are all data received from the field, customer reports, installation reports, etc., analysed to supplement in-house quality information?		Collaboration between Quality and Marketing ineffective
6. Are all scrap tickets and re-work tickets and quality-cost reports analysed to determine key areas for defect-prevention work?		Quality-cost reporting and analysis good
7. Are clear, readily understandable and carefully designed forms used for defect reporting?		
8. Are defect-trend charts prepared for all products for use by the unit quality improvement team, and its working groups?		For assembly and final test
9. Are clear trend charts prepared, highlighted and updated weekly for management giving defect levels at key stages in product manufacture?		Too many data supplied - not well presented
10. Is a quality status report prepared and distributed each month?		

FIGURE 4.7 **Example of rating sheet for quality-system audit**

TABLE 4.2

Questions for Rating Sheet for "Product Qualification and Re-Qualification

1 Are all major new products subjected to formal product qualification before release for sales and manufacturing?
Are the time, money and staff needed for the tests budgeted in the technical development programme?

2 Are all the requirements of each product, including performance, reliability and environmental capability fully specified by Technical?
Are the qualification tests performed exactly to defined qualification specifications which reflect the requirement specifications?
Are the qualification test specifications formally issued by Technical after approval by Technical and Quality?

3 Do the qualification tests include:
(i) functional performance test;
(ii) operation at limits of input voltages, etc.;
(iii) configuration check against approved drawings;
(iv) visual inspection of workmanship to defined standards and AQLs;[1]
(v) tests of environmental capability;
(vi) tests of reliability to the full extent practicable?

4 Are the tests carried out by technically competent staff in Technical and Quality or in an independent laboratory?

5 Does Quality accept full responsibility for auditing the tests and guaranteeing their objectivity and for auditing the proper logging of all test events and results?
Does Quality prepare status reports for management information?

6 Does Quality prepare a final qualification test report including a clear summary of the major conclusions for management action?

7 Does Technical have an effective system for implementing all changes to the product design indicated necessary by the test results?
Does Manufacturing have an effective system for implementing all changes to the manufacturing methods indicated necessary by the test results?

8 Has Quality a system for auditing and reporting on the corrective action of 7.

9 Are additional qualification tests performed to confirm that corrective actions taken have achieved their purpose? Are time and money budgeted for this work?

10 Is product requalification required on a periodic scheduled basis?
Are requalification tests being performed as required?

[1] See Chapter 6, page 95

elements high percentages will be obtained on average and in others low. In this way a summary of the strengths and weaknesses of the quality system is obtained. An arbitrary limit, e.g. 70 per cent, can be defined, special attention being given to elements receiving ratings less than the limit. Obviously, the level of marking is partially subjective and is dependent upon the judgement of the auditor. Consequently, no particular significance can be attached to the quantitative ratings—their purpose is to concentrate attention for the next stage of the audit.

It is not to be expected that even a very good quality system would give high ratings for each element. For a particular unit some of the elements may be of small importance or even completely irrelevant. The results of the rating should be reviewed by the auditor (if external) with the quality manager and his staff and agreement should be reached on which of the elements require improvement and an initial plan for action should be prepared. A short but clearly written report giving the results of the audit and the proposed and agreed actions should be prepared by the auditor. The quality manager should then discuss this report with the unit general manager, together with the auditor, with the purposes of familiarizing the general manager with the results of the audit and of getting his agreement to the action plan.

The writer's experience is that to carry out such an audit, including writing the report and discussing it with the general manager, takes about a week of full-time work for the auditor and the unit quality manager, and shorter periods for the other managers involved. Obviously the actual time will be dependent upon the size and complexity of the unit, whether it is engaged in the full range of activities considered—marketing, development, etc.—and whether more than one site is involved.

ZERO DEFECTS

Without doubt the most controversial topic that has been discussed within the field of quality control during the past decade has been the so-called zero-defects programme. It was first introduced in the Orlando division of the Martin Marietta company in 1961, the initial idea coming from P. B. Crosby. The Martin-Marietta work was described in the book *Zero Defects* by James Halpin and Crosby has developed the idea further in his book *Cutting the Cost of Quality*. Since then the methods of zero defects have been widely applied in many different industries in the USA and also in many other countries. There is a very active American Society for Zero Defects and the overall system has been endorsed by the USA Department of Defense (Crosby himself was given a special award by the Department for his work in the initiation of zero defects).

Many people, particularly professional workers in quality control, are opposed to zero defects. They attack it on a number of grounds. They claim that it is simply a worker-motivation programme and that as such it must be ineffective, because they say, quite rightly, that solution of most product-conformance problems rests with management, not workers. Further, it is the nature of motivation programmes that they produce short-term advantages, but these are lost as interest wanes. The critics also claim that zero defects is conceptually impossible, that any persistent attempt to approach that goal must be ruinously expensive and that it is incompatible with professional quality-control techniques such as the establishment of optimum AQLs (see Chapter 6). Many quality-control workers feel most at ease when engaged in the manipulation of statistics, the solution of specific hardware problems, the supervision of inspectors and testers, the development of test equipment and such-like activities. They feel inexperienced and insecure when required by the zero-defects programme to perform a new range of activities. They therefore attack it as "gimmicky", "typical American ballyhoo", and "quite incompatible with our national temperament".

The writer does not believe that a lengthy rebuttal of these objections is very fruitful. Briefly, Crosby emphasizes that the motivational aspects of zero defects are directed at management, not at workers—"ZD is a standard of management excellence." If management becomes convinced of the importance of having high standards, of having a resolution to perform every task properly, and knows that it is responsible for setting these standards, much of the rest will follow. For each work element the mental attitude and the planning must be to perform it without defect. But it does *not* follow from this that it can be assumed that the intention will always be realized either immediately or even in the long term. There is therefore no illogicality in performing inspection or setting AQLs in a zero defects context.

Top management is usually positive towards zero defects, recognizing intuitively where it will assist them to meet their personal goals, even if these are not explicitly the same as those of the programme. The workers themselves are invariably positive, because it adds interest to their activities, upgrades the value they themselves place on their work and provides a needed means of communication with their supervisors. A bonus that has surprised the organizers of many zero-defects programmes is that the staff turnover rate, i.e. the rate at which workers leave to get new jobs, is markedly reduced—in some cases by as much as 30 or 40 per cent.

The main argument for zero defects is that it works—the level of conformance of product improves and quality costs fall. As noted at the beginning of the chapter, the writer has been involved to a greater or less degree with quality-improvement programmes involving zero defects in the UK, France, Germany, Italy, Spain, and Belgium, and in each there were important and measurable improvements.

The essence of a zero-defects programme is that it must be carried out as part of a serious, long-term quality-improvement activity. Attempted as an isolated, single activity it is virtually certain to be received with cynicism by both workers and those members of management not directly involved in the decision to start, and any benefits are likely to be small and ephemeral. Performed as part of an overall quality-improvement programme it will be received with respect and provide benefits difficult to achieve by other means.

The intention to include zero defects as part of the quality-improvement programme will often be established at the initial, management-commitment stage. In fact, the zero-defect idea may be an important factor in realizing the management interest that is essential to a worthwhile commitment. Without it the programme, although worthy and useful, may be too dull to establish the necessary level of management enthusiasm. In other cases there may be no firm intention to carry out the ZD steps when the programme is started and its usefulness may become apparent when the quality-cost reporting and quality-measurement steps are achieved and there is a need for greater drive on corrective action and to extend participation in quality improvement beyond those involved as specialists.

The zero-defects programme is deliberately brought to a peak on ZD day and the necessity to work towards this is used as a spur to effective action by the various managers and departments involved in the preceding steps. The interest built up by ZD day and the involvement it gives of everyone in the whole unit are then used to achieve further benefits in the steps subsequent to ZD day.

Planning for ZD day is carried out by the inter-departmental quality-improvement team. It is important that it should not be scheduled too early. Many weeks and even months of quality measurement and quality-cost information should be available and should have been displayed throughout the various shops, offices and laboratories of the unit. At the same time it should have become clear throughout the unit that there was a sincere and energetic management drive towards quality improvement, evidenced at least as much by effective corrective-action activities as by the quality-awareness programme.

With the setting of the date for ZD day, the quality-improvement team can start the detailed planning of how it is to be handled. There are only a few rules. First, it is best that everyone in the unit is involved virtually simultaneously. If ZD day is held at different times for different groups, people not involved initially will hear about it from colleagues who are, and will wonder why they are being neglected. And the advantages of having a clearly defined high point in the programme will be lost.

A second key point is that all supervision in every department must be involved in the planning, must have a clear idea of the concepts involved and the methods to be used and must be wholeheartedly behind the programme. There should be no difficulty with this if the earlier steps have been performed well: if they have not, supervisors may be sceptical of management's real interest in quality and this scepticism will inevitably be passed on. Training of supervisors in the part they are to play in zero defects is therefore of key importance. There is much material available for this purpose in the form of films, tape recordings and brochures.

The unions must also participate. In all countries where the programme has been applied it has been found that the unions have had a predisposition towards zero defects. They appreciate the emphasis that it places upon the worth and value of the activities of their members.

In the original Martin Company ZD programme, and in many subsequent programmes in the USA, the method used to give simultaneous involvement of everyone in the unit was the use of a single-page explanation of the concept incorporating in it "the pledge". A typical example of this sheet is given in Figure 4.8. The way the document is used is as follows. The unit prepares copies of it on its letter-headed paper—one for each employee. The general manager of the unit retains them all. On ZD day he discusses the concept and pledge with all of the people who report to him directly. When all questions have been answered each member of the staff present signs his copy of the pledge and the general manager countersigns. The papers are then kept by the subordinates and each takes enough copies of the paper for every member of his department. He then repeats the procedure with those who report to him, and so on until every person in the unit has discussed the ZD concept with his direct supervisor and has signed the pledge with him. This method makes sure that every person gets the message: it also ensures that the management understands it. Signing the pledge is, of course, voluntary, but in the USA experience has been that, as part of a properly conducted quality-improvement programme, there has been a general willingness to sign.

In Europe the pledge has usually been omitted. Whether this reflects an accurate assessment of cultural differences between Americans and Europeans or simply a failure of nerve in the organizers of European programmes is not certain. Without the pledge the method is similar. The concept is explained in a single-page letter from the general manager to every employee and the method of distribution is exactly the same as when the pledge is used. Provided each supervisor treats the matter as important and deals effectively with discussion of the

INTERNATIONAL TELEPHONE AND TELEGRAPH CORPORATION
320 Park Avenue
New York. N.Y. 10022

ZERO DEFECTS - THE CONCEPT

Zero Defects is a performance standard. It is the standard of the craftsman regardless of his assignment. It is not limited to production efforts, in fact some of the largest gains are obtained from the "service" areas. The theme of ZD: DO IT RIGHT THE FIRST TIME. It means concentrate on preventing defects rather than detecting.

People are conditioned to believe that error is inevitable, thus they not only accept error, they anticipate it. It does not bother us to make a few errors in our work whether we are designing circuits, setting up a machine, soldering joints, typing letters or assembling components. "To err is human." We all have our own standard at which errors begin to bother us. It is better to get an "A" in school, but you still pass with a "C".

We do not maintain this same standard, however, when it comes to our personal life. If we did, we should expect to get shortchanged every now and then when we cash our paycheck; we should expect hospital nurses to drop a constant percentage of the newborn babies; we should resign ourselves to going home to the wrong house periodically, by mistake. We as individuals do not tolerate these things. We have a dual standard: one for ourselves, and one for our work.

Most human error is caused by lack of attention rather than lack of knowledge. Lack of attention is created when we assume that error is inevitable. If we consider this condition carefully, and pledge ourselves to make a constant conscious effort to do our job right the first time, we will take a giant step toward eliminating the waste of rework, scrap and repair that increases cost and reduces individual opportunity. Success is a journey, not a destination.

Let's set our sights on Zero Defects.

ZERO DEFECTS - THE PLEDGE

I freely pledge myself to make a constant, conscious effort to do my job right the first time recognizing that my individual contribution is a vital part of the overall effort.

____

____

FIGURE 4.8 **Example of the "pledge"**

concept the absence of the pledge does not seem seriously to reduce the effect.

On the same day, for the first time publicity is given to ZD by posters and by other methods such as special ZD lunches at reduced prices in the unit's restaurants and canteens.

It is also very useful to invite distinguished visitors to participate in the day, for example a principal member of local government such as the mayor, a director of a major customer, senior officials of the union and, where the unit is part of a larger company, the managing director of the whole company. Where it is planned to get all employees together for a further explanation of zero defects these visitors would be asked to give short speeches. Where this is not practicable, they should be invited to tour the factory, to see individual supervisors explaining the concept and discussing it with their staff. Of course, photographs are taken for articles in the company newspaper and the local newspaper also will usually be glad to give a report of the occasion.

ZD day provides a focal point for the whole quality-improvement programme and establishes an attitude environment for both management and workers in which progress is made easier.

Goal-Setting, Error-cause Removal and Recognition

Three further steps of the quality-improvement programme give the follow-up to ZD day. These are "goal-setting", "error-cause removal" and "recognition". About a week after ZD day individual supervisors should ask their people what quality-improvement goals they wish to set for themselves. Every area should produce goals and these should be specific and measurable: for example, reduce defects per unit by 20 per cent in one month. These goals should be posted in conspicuous places. Obviously, the previously established quality-measurement system provides a good tool for defining the goals and measuring progress. The goals should not be for increases in output—they should be concerned with reduction of defects and errors. Of course, output will accelerate as scrap, re-work and inspection are reduced.

Goal-setting is most effective when it is done by the personnel themselves, rather than if the goals are suggested by the supervisor. However, the latter should have some ideas in mind before the start of the discussion and should make sure that the tasks agreed are not too easy.

Goal-setting is not limited to production areas. Every engineering, accounting, purchasing, production-control, marketing and other group should establish goals related to performing their own work without error. In this respect the zero-defects programme is *not* limited to activities which have a direct bearing on product quality. It gives an opportunity of introducing the quality-control ideas of "doing the job right the first time" and of establishing methods of measuring quantitatively defect or error levels, so that progress can be followed, into departments and functions where these concepts are not normally applied explicitly. Error levels, measured for the first time for this purpose, are often high and therefore give important improvement opportunities.

Another particular technique applied after ZD day to sustain interest and activity for defect prevention is the error-cause removal programme. In this all workers are encouraged to define the causes of their own errors and to communicate them to their supervisors. To do this, simple one-page forms are provided in every area, usually in wall boxes. When an employee recognizes that he has a problem he completes the form and drops it in the box. The system must then be such that the employee is quickly notified that the problem is under investigation, and, of course, the problem must be passed to the department responsible for its solution. Studies of ECR programmes show that 90 per cent of the causes of error identified are acted upon and the majority of these are solved by the first level of supervision. The error-cause removal programme must include a method of keeping track of each identified item, to ensure that the necessary corrective action is taken or that it is formally decided that no effective action can be taken. In the latter case the next higher level of supervision must be involved, as a discipline against problems being sidetracked. Problems must be dealt with quickly and the employees concerned must be kept informed of progress.

The error-cause removal programme provides a means of communication between employees and management that is often missing. Without an ECR programme employees put up with difficulties that they know mitigate against error-free work, because they do not feel they are important enough to bother their supervisor with. An ECR programme breaks down this barrier and, in the receptive environment created by ZD day, produces a flood of useful ideas.

Error-cause removal programmes are obviously similar in many respects to suggestion schemes. They differ in two respects: the primary emphasis is on quality and the prevention of errors and the employee is not required to suggest a solution to his problem—this is the responsibility of the appropriate department (which will usually prefer its own solution anyway). Of course, the employee is not prevented from suggesting a solution and if this is adopted the employee will get the appropriate reward for a successful suggestion.

Because organizationally an ECR programme is similar to a suggestion scheme, it is not at all difficult to run. Even when applied as an isolated activity an ECR programme can give important benefits. However, it is much better for it to be part of a sustained ZD activity which in turn is part of a long-term quality-improvement programme.

A very important part of the zero-defects activity is to give "recognition" to employees who, both singly and in groups, have made significant achievements in defect prevention. Achievements can be related to quality-improvement goals or defining important causes of error and so on. ZD is a completely voluntary activity so that particularly energetic or effective actions merit appreciation and recognition from management. The type of recognition that should be used is, for example, to have the activity form the subject of an article in the company newspaper. Another method is for a senior manager to give congratulations personally in the presence of the rest of the department. Special lunches or dinners are another good method of recognizing the achievements of a particularly efficient group.

The quality-improvement team should develop flexible recognition methods that are appropriate to the company. They should not consist mainly of handing out trinkets—this will only serve to devalue the importance of the programme. People work for appreciation, not a ball-point pen.

The fourteenth step of the quality-improvement programme is concerned with quality councils and these have already been discussed in Chapter 3. Obviously in a multi-unit company discussion at the quality council can be a very effective way of exchanging information on the best ways of carrying out the quality-improvement programme. It can also be extremely useful in building up the confidence of members of the council to start some of the more difficult steps of the programme.

The use of the integrated quality-improvement programme is one of the most important quality-control advances to have been developed in the past ten years. Most of the activities involved are simple and straightforward and do not require any difficult techniques. However, they are not to be despised for this simplicity. The combination of management commitment and standard setting, participation of *all* departments and the involvement of the entire personnel is the most effective way yet invented of getting major quality improvement.

5 The Quality Department and the General Manager

Quality control has changed with the passage of time. In the past it was mainly an inspection and test activity, concerned with preventing defective product leaving the factory and with assisting re-work. Later the specialized techniques of statistical quality control in sampling, process-proving, machine-capability studies, process control, etc., were added. In neither of these phases was there any pressing need for regular and direct communication between the quality people and the general manager. The chief inspector would only talk to the general manager about specific product matters at times of trouble. If the trouble was from a customer the general manager might tell the chief inspector to be "tougher" or say, "Why don't you shut the line down?" If the trouble was failure to meet the schedule the instruction might be, "Stop being so fussy about details. The stuff works doesn't it?" But usually the situation was quiet and there was no need for communication. There was even less communication between the general manager and the statistical quality-control experts. The latter, if competent, did an important job in a specialized way, but it impacted only indirectly on the primary interests of the general manager, and in a way not easily understood by him.

The demands on quality control in modern, competitive industry can only be met if there is understanding and effective communication between general management and the quality department. Without this it is difficult to progress beyond inspection, test and statistical techniques.

Much of the emphasis of modern quality control is on measuring and reporting. The final purposes are to ensure the customers get conforming products and that quality costs are minimized, but the immediate purpose is often to clarify the inadequacies of other departments in meeting their quality responsibilities. The aim is to establish a system in which engineering designs conforming products, purchasing buys conforming parts, manufacturing makes conforming products and so on. And to ensure that this happens there has to be continual measuring and reporting of the degree of success.

The overall defect-prevention activities described in the previous chapter on the quality-improvement programme and in subsequent chapters on the quality control of purchased goods, and of new products, will only work effectively with the support and participation of the general manager. He in turn can use the quality department as a means of knowing the quality situation and of exercising pressure on the other departments. This requires honest, objective and clear reporting from the quality department. The general manager must know that he can certainly trust information from that source and that it is not diminished because of fear, exaggerated for excitement or twisted to escape blame. He must support and protect the quality department and not make it responsible for the quality deficiencies of other departments. Apart from being unjust this will inevitably muffle the flow of honest information.

The establishment of effective communication between the quality department and general management is very difficult, but very important. Sometimes the quality manager will not be invited to the general manager's staff meetings. Often the quality manager's reports will be incomprehensible.

QUALITY REPORTS

One of the principal means of communication from the quality manager to the general manager is the regular quality report, monthly or weekly. This should cover two main areas. It should deal with specific, important events that are current during the reporting period. These are likely to be either major accomplishments or major problems. It should also report on the progress of important quality programmes of a continuing nature, such as quality-cost reduction programmes, quality-manpower control programmes, the implementation of the steps of the quality-improvement programme, and the progress of the reduction of defect levels. The report will contain written material and tables and graphs, but it should be short—not more than three or four pages. For each problem the actions being taken to overcome it must be given, the name of the person responsible and the scheduled date for completion of the solution. Table 5.1 gives a check list of topics for the quality report. In the current section only

TABLE 5.1

Contents of the Quality Report

Topic	Method of Presentation
Current Events	
Major customer complaint	written
Important test or inspection rejection with schedule and cost impact	written
Test or inspection hold-up due to lack of quality manpower or facilities	written
Decision to order important piece of test equipment	written
Major cost reduction in quality area	written
Completion of particular step of the quality-improvement programme	written
Pass or fail of qualification test on new product	written
Design review results on new product	written
Results of system quality audit	written
Continuing Programmes	
Progress against quality-cost reduction targets	tabular and written comment
Progress on quality manpower-control programme	tabular and written comment
Completion of scheduled quality-improvement steps	tabular and written comment
Reduction of product-defect levels	graphical and written comment
Progress on supplier-control programme	written
Quality Manager's Overview	written

particular events happening in the reporting period should be dealt with. The report should not be padded with negative information. For the continuing programmes tabular and graphical material should be updated in each report and written comment must be given where there is any departure from the planned programmes, e.g. if the budgeted quality-cost reduction is not achieved. The report should conclude with a brief overview in which the quality manager gives his *opinion* of the situation.

Quality reports often consist largely of a whole series of graphs depicting defect levels at different stages on various products. Such information is a proper part of a quality report to the general manager, but the volume must be kept under control, the clarity of presentation must be good and it must be completely self-explanatory. No more than two or three pages of such graphs should be given. This can be achieved by including only the most important products, or products showing improvements or deteriorations. It is not necessary to report on the same products in each report. The temptation to combine results in incomprehensible quality indices (see Chapter 4) must be resisted.

Targets for Quality-cost Reduction and Quality-manpower Control

As a part of the annual planning and budgeting programme the general manager should establish targets for reduction of quality costs and control of quality manpower for his unit. Clear action programmes to enable the reductions to be achieved, and following the standard quality-improvement programme, must also be established. The quality-cost reduction target and the actions to achieve it apply to the unit as a whole and are not restricted to the quality department. In fact most of the initial actions must come from other departments: Purchasing in better control of bought components; Engineering in better specification and testing of new products; Manufacturing in making the product "right the first time" and so on. However, as other departments improve, the amount of inspection and test needed for screening out defective product and for assisting re-work must diminish. Where activity is expanding this means that a constant level of inspection and test manpower can deal with a greater volume of product, but where it is not, the inspection and test manpower must be run down. If this is not done an important part of the improvement will be lost.

When quality costs are correctly measured according to the methods described in Chapter 2, for much of manufacturing industry the quality costs will be eight to ten per cent of sales. (The inspection and test manpower totalled from all departments is also often ten per cent or more of the total unit manpower.) The quality-cost ratio will depend upon the complexity of the product (the more complex the product the higher the quality costs) and the proportion of purchased parts and added value. A really effective, management-led drive on quality-cost reduction, with the emphasis on defect prevention from all departments, can eliminate up to half of those quality costs over a period of time. In the first year of the quality-improvement programme a reasonable target is to reduce the quality costs by ten to twenty per cent. A corresponding reduction in inspection and test manpower ratios should also be targeted.

This can give an enormous benefit to the profitability of the unit. For example, most companies would consider a net income to sales ratio (before tax) of ten per cent quite reasonable. If quality costs also are ten per cent of sales, any reduction in quality costs gives a proportional increase in return on sales. Say the improvement programme reduces quality costs by fifteen per cent, then the return on sales should increase by the same amount. Over three or four years the quality-improvement programme, without any major capital or other expenditure, could increase the return on sales from ten per cent to fourteen or fifteen per cent. The general manager running such a programme will use the quality report and the quality-cost report as a means of regularly monitoring its progress.

At the same time the level of conformance of product going to the customer will actually improve—such is the effect of a well-run quality-improvement programme.

CONSOLIDATED QUALITY REPORT

Many companies have more than one operating group. They may have separate divisions making different product lines or two or more factories each with their own management. Some of the different organizations that can be involved have been discussed in Chapter 3. There is then a need for a quality report that consolidates the information contained in the individual unit reports. The consolidated quality report is written by the company quality director to the managing director. It will deal with the same kind of information as the unit reports—important current events, problems and achievements and a review of continuing programmes. It will use written and tabular presentations, but will not normally include graphs of product defect levels.

It is an important responsibility of the company quality director to determine how the company shall be divided into units for the purpose of quality reporting. The same division must be used for the production of quality-cost reports, although these are produced by the unit comptrollers, and the same division will also be used for the planning and budgeting of the quality activities of the company. The quality director must obtain the agreement of division and plant managers and the company comptroller for the reporting pattern.

Figure 5.1 shows an example of the cover page of a consolidated quality report. On an A4 size sheet of paper it enables the up-to-date quality-cost situation of every unit in the company to be summarized and also gives room for a brief account of the two or three most important problems and accomplishments of the company in the quality area.

CONSOLIDATED QUALITY REPORT

TO A. Vincent ..... MONTH REPORTED November 1970

COMPANY ACB ..... DATE SUBMITTED December 15, 1970

ADDRESS Paris ..... PREPARED BY B. Pauthier

I QUALITY COSTS

			UNIT								
			Cable	Inst.	Trans.	Switch					
QUALITY COST AS % OF SALES	PREVIOUS YEAR		4.70	10.5	7.01	3.62					
	ACTUAL 1970 YEAR TO DATE	J	6.02	11.0	6.75	5.29					
		F	4.74	12.3	7.68	4.37					
		M	4.86	13.1	8.27	4.22					
		A	4.55	13.0	8.50	4.09					
		M	4.59	12.0	8.51	4.07					
		J	4.53	11.5	7.40	3.91					
		J	4.57	11.3	7.28	3.94					
		A	4.64	11.3	7.53	3.99					
		S	4.61	11.1	7.59	4.02					
		O	4.62	11.2	7.71	4.02					
		N									
		D									
	TARGET (YEAR)		4.60	13.4	6.26	3.38					TOTALS
$ 000'S YEAR TO DATE	SALES	ACTUAL	15,9	8,55	10,9	38,1					73,5
		BUDGET	15,0	7,75	12,0	38,1					72,8
	QUALITY COST	ACTUAL	735	960	840	1,53					4,07
		VAR (PR. YR.)	12.7	(60)	(76.5)	(152)					(276)
		VAR (TAR)	(3.18)	188	(158)	(244)					(217)

II MAJOR ACCOMPLISHMENTS AND MAJOR PROBLEMS

FIGURE 5.1 **Consolidated quality report—cover page**

In the quality-cost table the emphasis is upon the quality cost divided by sales, given as a percentage. In some companies it may be better to use quality cost divided by added cost (see Chapter 2). The target for the year is established in terms of the quality-cost to sales percentage and progress is measured using it. However, information is also given in money terms, so that the financial magnitude of progress or deterioration in each unit is immediately apparent. The year-to-date quality cost is given, the £ variance against the previous year and also the £ variance against the target for the end of the current year. Figures indicating a deterioration or failure to meet target are given in brackets. The variances of quality cost (QC) against previous year (Pr. Yr.) and against target (Tar.) for the year to date (YTD) are calculated using the following equations, which were discussed in Chapter 2.

$$\text{Variance (Pr. Yr.) £000's} = \left[\left(\frac{\text{QC}}{\text{Sales}}\right)_{\text{Pr.Yr.}} - \left(\frac{\text{QC}}{\text{Sales}}\right)_{\text{YTD}}\right] \text{Sales YTD £000's}$$

$$\text{Variance (Tar.) £000's} = \left[\left(\frac{\text{QC}}{\text{Sales}}\right)_{\text{YTD}} - \left(\frac{\text{QC}}{\text{Sales}}\right)_{\text{Tar.}}\right] \text{Sales YTD £000's}$$

The quality-cost table contains the year-to-date figures, not the figures for the individual months, because these are what are needed to calculate the variances. It is also necessary to give the percentages to two decimal places, e.g. 6·72 per cent, to get the required accuracy. These equations appear complicated, but they need to be understood in detail only by the quality-department staff responsible for completing this part of the consolidated quality report. Readers of the table can immediately see, for each unit, whether or not the quality-cost to sales percentage is reducing from the previous-year value towards the planned year-end target. They can also see how much money is being saved compared to last year and whether this is as much as planned. The information on actual and budgeted sales is also useful because, for reasons of fixed overhead, it is easier to achieve a reduction in the quality-cost to sales percentage if sales are over budget and harder if they are under.

The sales, quality costs and variances for the individual units should be added up to give the company result. The company variances should *not* be obtained by applying the equations to the total company quality costs and sales. A different result will be obtained, which has less meaning. The quality-cost savings are made by actions performed in the units and the sum of these gives the best representation of the overall company position. The summations should be made even if some units have not reported or are out of date, but the sales total should only include the sales of units reporting quality costs. For this reason the sales given in the quality-cost table may be less than the actual sales of the company.

Figure 5.2 gives another very useful table in which the total quality manpower of the company can be summarized unit by unit. This table must cover all staff engaged in quality activities including people

III HEADCOUNT			UNIT								TOTALS
			Cable	Inst.	Trans	Switch					
TOTAL QC, INSP AND TEST	PREVIOUS YEAR		51	188	208	493					940
	END 197 QUARTERS	1	54	198	229	518					999
		2	53	207	211	541					1012
		3	53	214	206	550					1023
		4									
AS % OF TOTAL MANFG. AND INSTLN.	PREVIOUS YEAR		7.95	12.7	22.2	14.7					14.2
	END 197 QUARTERS	1	8.17	14.0	24.4	14.9					14.6
		2	7.77	14.8	24.0	15.3					14.9
		3	7.90	14.7	23.6	15.4					14.9
		4									
	TARGET		7.80	-	24.5	15.5					18.6
AS % OF TOTAL UNIT	PREVIOUS YEAR		7.50	13.5	18.5	13.1					11.7
	END 197 QUARTERS	1	7.93	13.8	20.1	13.3					12.1
		2	7.55	14.4	19.4	13.5					12.2
		3	7.63	14.4	18.9	13.6					12.2
		4									
	TARGET		7.56	12.0	19.4	13.6					11.8

FIGURE 5.2 **Consolidated quality report—manpower summary**

doing inspection and test who are not members of the quality department, e.g. in the manufacturing and installation departments. The number should be the same as that used in calculating prevention and appraisal costs as part of the quality-cost reporting. Headcount does not usually change very rapidly so it is sufficient to complete this table every quarter year. The figures given refer to the end of the designated period: the end of the previous year, the end of the current quarter year, etc.

As for quality costs, the targets established as part of the business-planning and budgeting process are done in terms of ratios—in this case in terms of the total manufacturing and installation headcount (usually *including* the quality headcount) and the total unit headcount.

Control of quality headcount is an important cross-check on the quality-cost results. It is difficult for the quality costs to improve without a headcount change. Setting targets for quality headcount ratios also emphasizes that, as the product improves because of defect-prevention activities, it requires less inspection and test.

QUALITY DEPARTMENT RECRUITING AND TRAINING

In this book the modern role of the quality department is described. This role requires that the senior members of the department are an integral part of the management team of the whole unit. It requires the staff of the quality department to work effectively on terms of equality with their colleagues in other departments. Quality management must give leadership in quality-improvement programmes, in purchased-material improvement programmes, in qualification testing and so on. They must participate effectively in design-review activities—and they must really communicate with general management. None of this is possible if the members of the quality department are clearly of lower intellectual calibre and managerial skill and energy than members of other departments.

Unfortunately, there is no automatic progression that provides people of high calibre for quality departments. Universities, colleges of technology and other institutes of higher education produce a continual stream of engineering and science graduates, many of whom enter industry. However the majority wish to go into research, development or design engineering. These departments are therefore customarily well stocked with intelligent, ambitious young men. A smaller group will have graduated in industrial engineering and will naturally gravitate to the appropriate parts of the manufacturing department. The accountants have their own methods of recruiting and training people of high calibre and these days arts graduates are frequently turning to marketing.

Other important departments including purchasing, production control and quality have a much more difficult problem in recruitment. This is because higher education has two aspects: intellectual and vocational. To satisfy the first requirement the subject studied must have a magnitude and complexity sufficient to expand and develop the mind of the student and to help him to gain an understanding of some major aspect of the cultural life of his own civilization. The basic physical sciences, chemistry, physics, etc., the humanities, history, the study of the language and literature of foreign countries, the major engineering disciplines and many others are subjects appropriate to this basic educational requirement. Clearly purchasing, production control and quality control are not. Even if padded with irrelevancies these subjects are not suitable vehicles for general education at a high level.

A young man who has studied chemistry for educational reasons will also have acquired much knowledge and technique of vocational use, and will be very likely to exploit this by entering research and development in the chemical industry. Vocations of this kind therefore have a great advantage in recruiting staff of high potential compared with non-educational vocations.

The consequence of this situation is that top-calibre staff will not enter Quality automatically. Typical entrants to quality departments are:

(*a*) young girls with no educational qualification, as mechanical inspectors;

(*b*) married women with perhaps some "O-levels", as statistical clerks;

(*c*) older men transferring from production, as inspectors or inspection supervisors;

(*d*) young men studying for ONC on day release, as electrical testers;

(*e*) young men having ONC and studying for HNC on day release, as test engineers.

Staff of higher potential than this will only enter Quality if there is a concentrated management programme to induce them to do so. Usually there is no such programme, or at best it may consist of transferring-in some known "losers" from Engineering, or providing a quiet haven for a respected chief engineer in his last few years before retirement. (That is not to say that an energetic and quality-minded chief engineer, released at an earlier stage of his career by some organizational upheaval, may not make a very good quality manager.)

What is required is a programme for *promoting* young graduates from Engineering into responsible positions in the quality department. These men are unlikely to be the most creative design engineers, but they should have the necessary technical and personal qualities successfully to carry responsibility in their new department. Experience shows that when this is done these engineers often earn another promotion within two or three years. A modern quality department, because it interacts with virtually all other departments and also suppliers and customers, provides an extremely rich experience for a young engineer. Because competition is less than in development departments, his opportunities for accepting real responsibility at an early age are higher. Usually, when such an engineer is promoted out of the quality department he leaves a major gap. The answer to this, of course, is not to block such promotions but to ensure that enough competent young engineers enter the department.

As noted above, good-calibre people will not automatically enter the Quality department. The general manager, persuaded by his quality manager, must determine that it shall happen by creating the policy, by providing the budget (easily recovered by the quality-cost reduction programme), by approving the vacancies and by establishing the conditions in which other departments can release staff. The general manager must also demand that the quality department fulfils its modern role and therefore needs good staff.

A good quality engineer or manager requires expertise in several different areas. He needs a basic level of technical knowledge of the product with which he is dealing. If he has come from the engineering department this will be no problem. Otherwise he should take part in training programmes designed for the development engineers. He should also have an understanding of statistical quality control. There are many good, part-time courses at technical colleges which will provide this expertise in a few months and many books that can be studied privately. The key management and communication skills may have to be learnt on the job, although there are occasional one or two week courses on quality management and utilizing case studies, which can be useful in this area.

6 Inspection by Sampling

More has been written about statistical quality control than about any other aspect of the control of quality. The writer believes that the reasons for this are historical and practical. Historical because the first people working at quality control who were intellectually likely to write books were the professional statisticians. Practically, because statistical quality control, with its specific techniques and mathematical background lends itself more readily than other branches of quality control to formal teaching and a set of lecture notes forms a natural basis for a book. In recent years the balance has been corrected to some extent by the publication of books emphasizing the managerial aspects of quality control.

This chapter is the only one in this book concerned with statistical quality control. No attempt is made to deal even briefly with the wide range of statistical techniques applicable to quality, most of which, in practice, are used infrequently. Instead the chapter is devoted to inspection by sampling, which is a technique which is applied universally, although often inefficiently and with little understanding of its logical basis. A simple description of the mathematics of attribute sampling is given, but the chapter is mainly devoted to a discussion of the place of sampling inspection in the overall system of production, inspection and corrective action. Technical variations of sampling such as double, multiple and sequential sampling and the complexities of AOQ, AOQL and LQ are not discussed. LQ is similar in some respect to LTPD which is discussed later (see page 95). These terms are well covered in guides to sampling tables (e.g. DG 7A published by the UK Ministry of Defence). Another topic which is not covered is sampling by "variables": it is simply recorded that the most widely used variables sampling plan is MIL–STD–414 published by the US Department of Defense.

ONE HUNDRED PER CENT INSPECTION

In sampling inspection only a fraction, the sample, of the items under consideration is inspected, Thus sampling inspection is differentiated from 100 per cent inspection in which every item under consideration is inspected.

Some of the reasons for carrying out inspections and tests have been touched upon in Chapter 2, as part of the discussion of quality costs. In full the reasons are as follows:

(i) to separate defective[1] product from non-defective product;

(ii) to identify the defects in defective product so that the product can be re-worked or scrapped;

(iii) to measure the defect level in the product to assist decision about whether the product will be sold (or whether it will be passed to a subsequent process);

(iv) to give information about the processes by which the product is made. This information is used to help control the level of defects in product made subsequently to the test or inspection (i.e. "prevention").

In comparing sampling inspection and 100 per cent inspection it is important to be aware that 100 per cent inspection is not usually performed with perfect accuracy. If four or five simple items are to be inspected, perfection may be expected. However, if many thousands of complex items are to be inspected, it is unlikely that a 100 per cent inspection will be done perfectly. For example, a manufacturer of semiconductor devices may make 100,000 or more of a particular transistor each week. 100 per cent testing of these devices will be carried out, possibly for ten or more characteristics (gain, frequency response, breakdown voltage, leakage current, etc.), each one of which may have an upper and lower failure limit. When account is taken of

[1] "A defective is a unit or product which contains one or more defects . . . "A defect is any non-conformance of the unit of product to specified requirements." (British Standard 9001: 1967).

The words defect, defective, imperfection, blemish, bug (as in de-bug), fault, failure, error, mistake are used in a fairly random and illogical manner by workers in quality control. The writer believes that the only such terms needed in quality control, in addition to defect and defective, are:

error: an error is a wrong action of a person, resulting in the production of one or more defects;

failure: a failure is an event occurring during a test (or use) when the unit does not perform according to its requirements. (Failure is also a term used in reliability—see Chapter 9.)

An error by a person leads to the production of a defective unit of product, which contains defects and gives rise to a failure during test. In practice, the other words are used as synonyms or combinations of these four terms.

human error, test-equipment deficiencies and instabilities of the devices under test, it is not surprising that lots of transistors, even after 100 per cent testing, commonly contain about 1 per cent of defective devices (i.e. devices not exactly to specification). Similarly, it has often been said that visual inspections are only 80 or 90 per cent efficient. This is an over simplification, but it certainly applies when the defects are not obvious and their proportion is low.

One hundred per cent inspection or test can be used for all four of the purposes listed above. However, it has one disadvantage for measuring the defect level for sentencing (purpose(iii)). This is that 100 per cent inspection, as normally performed, changes the defective level. The defective items found are usually scrapped or re-worked. The inspection measures the proportion that were defective in the lot submitted to inspection, but not that in the lot that goes to the customer after the defectives have been screened out. For example, a customer might agree to accept lots containing no more than 0·1 per cent of defective items. 100 per cent visual inspection of a lot of 10,000 items might reveal 140 defectives. After removal of the 140, does the lot still contain more than ten defectives and is it therefore rejectable? Unless the efficiency of the inspection is known the question cannot be answered without further inspection. This point is often neglected. A 100 per cent inspection is carried out and it is implicitly assumed that the product is then perfect. There is then some surprise when the customer complains that it is not.

The normal reasons for carrying out 100 per cent inspection or test are to screen out defective product and to assist re-work (purposes (i) and (ii)). It is not usual to perform 100 per cent inspection or test only to give quality information for defect-prevention purposes. However, if 100 per cent inspection or test is being carried out because of screening or re-work, addition of an accurate defect-reporting system enables the defect-prevention purpose to be realized also. Sometimes 100 per cent inspection or test is not utilized as a source of information and money is wasted carrying out a subsequent inspection or test especially to get defect information.

INSPECTION BY SAMPLING

A typical example of inspection or test by sampling is the following. A lot of 5,000 items of a particular product is collected together. The various attributes that each item must have for it to be acceptable are defined. For example, if the product was a resistor the attributes would include the allowed range of resistance, the physical dimensions, the legibility of the branding, the solderability of the leads, etc.

Methods of testing or inspecting for these characteristics would be defined. It might then be decided that the acceptability of the lot as a whole would be determined by inspecting and testing only a sample of the resistors, not all of the 5,000. A common way of doing this would be to take a sample of 200 of the resistors in a random manner from the 5,000 and subject the sample resistors to all the specified tests. If five or less of the 200 were found to be defective (i.e. did not have exactly the specified attributes) the lot of 5,000 would be accepted: if six or more were defective the lot would be rejected.

The reason for carrying out the inspections and tests is to enable the lot of 5,000 to be sentenced, i.e. it is an example of the third of the four purposes for carrying out inspection or test. The other main reason for carrying out a sampling inspection or test—for defect-prevention information—will be discussed later. It is clear that sampling cannot achieve the first two purposes of inspection and test. Inspecting 200 out of a lot of 5,000 does not effectively separate defective product from non-defective. If five defective items are found in the sample it is likely that the remaining 4,800 will contain 100 or so more defectives, but the sampling has left the vast majority of the defectives mixed with the non-defectives. Purpose (ii) is not achieved either: the sampling has not identified the defects in the 5,000 and re-work to correct them cannot take place.

Sampling can indirectly assist the achievement of the first two purposes. In our example it might have been decided that lots of resistors passing the sampling test and inspection would be shipped to the customer, whereas lots failing a test would be 100 per cent inspected or tested to separate out the defectives. (The lot should then be resampled to measure the achieved defective level.)

Because sampling does not enable defectives to be screened out, it does not significantly affect the quality of the lot inspected. In our example screening out five defectives gave only a trivial reduction in the total defective content of the 5,000. Unlike 100 per cent inspection, as noted above, it does not therefore suffer from this disadvantage when used as a method of measuring the defective level.

The above example includes the essential features of the use of attribute-sampling inspection or test for sentencing a lot of product. The required attributes of the product were defined. Methods of testing or inspecting for these attributes were specified. It was decided to take a sample of 200 from a lot of 5,000. It was decided that the lot would be accepted if five or less defectives were found in the sample and rejected if six or more were found. It is clear that all the information needed to enable the inspection to be carried out and the lots to be sentenced has been provided.

Theory of Attribute Sampling

In inspection or test of a product by attributes the items of product fall into two categories: "good" items that have *all* the required attributes and defective (bad) items that lack one or more of the required attributes. Attribute inspection or test is concerned only with good and bad items, so the theory of attribute sampling is fairly easy.

Consider a bag containing 100 balls with certain defined attributes. This is the lot. We now inspect these 100 per cent, or 200 per cent or more if necessary, for the defined attributes, so that we know exactly how many of the 100 balls are good and how many are defective. Suppose 30 are bad and 70 good.

If, without looking, we take one ball out of the bag and then inspect it the probability of its being bad is 0·3 and of its being good is 0·7.

Suppose we took a sample of five balls out of the lot in sequence and inspected each one in turn,[1] and found the first was bad, the second and third good, the fourth bad and the fifth good, i.e. BGGBG. The probability of getting this particular sequence is: 0·3 × 0·7 × 0·7 × 0·3 × 0·7. Multiplying this out gives 0·03087. If we continued to take samples of five balls out of the lot this particular sequence would appear about three times in every hundred samples.

BGGBG is only one of the ways of getting three good balls and two bad balls in a sample of five. In fact there are ten different sequences:

GGGBB	GBBGG
GGBBG	BBGGG
GGBGB	BGGGB
GBGGB	BGGBG
GBGBG	BGBGG

Each one of these sequences has a probability of 0·03087.

The probability of getting any one of these samples containing three good balls and two bad balls from the lot is therefore ten times the probability of getting a sample with one particular sequence. The probability of getting *any* arrangement of three good balls and two bad balls is therefore 10 × 0·03087 = 0·3087. If we continued to take samples of five balls out of the lot we would expect to get three good and two bad balls about thirty times in every hundred samples taken.

In the same way the probability of getting the sequence GGGBG, which includes only one bad ball, is given by: 0·7 × 0·7 × 0·7 × 0·3 × 0·7 = 0·07203. There are obviously five ways of placing one bad ball in a sample of five, so that if the order is unimportant the

[1] For exactness each ball should be returned to the lot after inspection so that the lot size from which item is taken remains 100.

probability of getting one bad ball in a sample of five taken from the lot is $5 \times 0{\cdot}07203 = 0{\cdot}36015$.

Similarly the probability of getting a sample containing entirely good balls is $0{\cdot}7^5 = 0{\cdot}16807$ and there is only one kind of sample like this.

In summary, if we take a sample of five balls from a lot containing 70 good and 30 bad balls we have the following probabilities of getting different numbers of bad balls:

Number of bad balls	0	1	2
Probability	$1 \times 0{\cdot}7^5$ 0·16807	$5 \times 0{\cdot}7^4 \times 0{\cdot}3$ 0·36015	$10 \times 0{\cdot}7^3 \times 0{\cdot}3^2$ 0·3087

Adding together 0·16807, 0·36015 and 0·3087 gives 0·83692. The remaining probability of 0·16308 is accounted for by the chances of getting 3, 4 and 5 bad balls. It is a certainty (probability = 1) that the sample of 5 balls will contain either 0, 1, 2, 3, 4, or 5 bad balls.

It was noted above that in carrying out sampling inspection it was necessary to decide what the sample size should be and the maximum number of defectives allowed in the sample for the lot still to be accepted (the latter is called the "acceptance number"). The properties of each sample size and acceptance number can be summarized in a graph of "probability of acceptance" against "lot per cent defective", and this graph is known as the "operating characteristic" of the sample size and acceptance number.

The operating characteristic for a sample size of 5 and an acceptance number of 1 is given in Figure 6.1. One point on this graph is marked with a small circle. This point shows that a lot that is 30 per cent defective has a probability of acceptance of 0·53. In other words, when a sample of 5 is taken from a lot that is 30 per cent defective there is a total probability of 0·53 that the sample will contain either no defectives, or one defective (i.e. satisfy an acceptance number of 1).

The calculations carried out earlier in this section showed that for a sample of 5 taken from a lot 30 per cent defective there was a probability of 0·16807 of getting no defectives and of 0·36015 of getting one defective. Together these sum to 0·52822. The calculation therefore gave the means of obtaining the point marked of the operating characteristic. Exactly the same calculation, but using percentage defectives other than 30, enables the rest of this operating characteristic to be calculated.

For practical sampling, inspection tables of operating characteristics are used to describe the properties of various pairs of sample sizes and acceptance numbers. The essential theoretical basis of the calculation of operating characteristics, and therefore of attribute sampling itself, is summarized above. Of course, to determine the operating characteristic of samples larger than 5 by the means described here would be impossibly tedious. Fortunately, the numbers 0·16807, 0·36015 and 0·3087 are the first three terms of the binomial $(0{\cdot}7 + 0{\cdot}3)^5$ and the known mathematical properties of this and similar binomials facilitate the calculation of operating characteristics. Two other mathematical relationships, the Poisson and hypergeometric distributions are also used in practice for calculating operating characteristics.

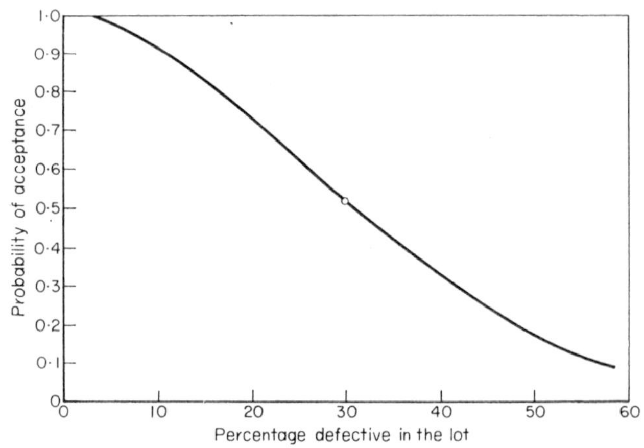

FIGURE 6.1 **Operating characteristic for a sample size of 5 and an acceptance number of 1**

It was noted above that to carry out attribute sampling it was necessary to define the required attributes of the product, the methods of test or inspection, the sample size and the acceptance number. With this information inspection can be carried out and lots accepted or rejected. Examination of the operating characteristic of the sample size and acceptance number enables the likely defective level of the accepted and rejected lots to be known.

Figure 6.1 gives the operating characteristic of a sample of 5 and an acceptance number of 1. It shows that lots which are 31 per cent defective have an even chance of being accepted or rejected by this sampling. It also shows that lots have to be as good as 11 per cent defective to have a probability of 0·9 of being accepted and as bad as 58 per cent defective to have a probability of 0·9 of being rejected. This means that lots which are better than 11 per cent defective are likely to be accepted, lots worse than 58 per cent defective are likely to be rejected and lots with a quality level between these figures may be either accepted or rejected. For most purposes this particular sampling plan gives an unsatisfactory method of determining whether lots are good or bad. The inadequacy arises from the smallness of the sample. Inspection of five items is likely to be very cheap, but does not give much information, and therefore provides a poor separation of good and bad.

Figure 6.2 shows the operating characteristic for a sample size of 50 and an acceptance number of 10, both numbers being ten times as large as for the previous example. For this sampling, lots which are

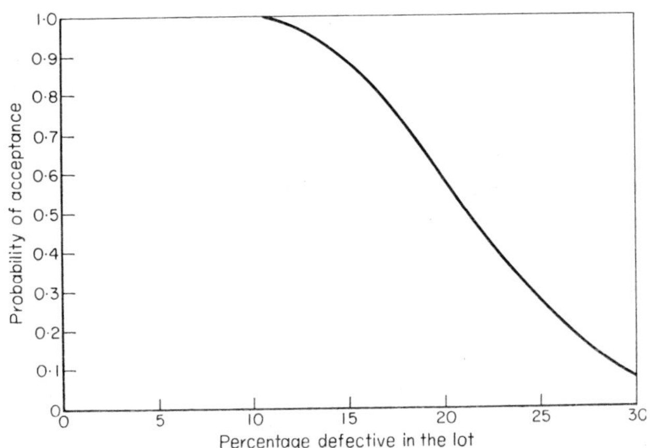

FIGURE 6.2 **Operating characteristic for a sample size of 50 and an acceptance number of 10**

21 per cent defective have an even chance of acceptance or rejection. Lots which are as good as 14·5 per cent defective have a probability of 0·9 of being accepted and lots which are as bad as 29 per cent defective have a probability of 0·9 of being rejected. By increasing the sample size from 5 to 50, the range of lot quality for which either acceptance or rejection is likely has been reduced from 11–58 per cent to 14·5–29 per cent.

Figure 6.3 gives the operating characteristic of one more sampling plan—sample size 80, acceptance number 2. For reasons which will be explained later, this is a more commonly used plan than either of the others discussed above. For this sampling there is an even chance of acceptance for lots which are 3·4 per cent defective, a probability of acceptance of 0·9 for lots which are as good as 1·4 per cent defective and a probability of rejection of 0·9 for lots which are as bad as 6·5 per cent defective. For this sampling plan the range of per cent defective for which either acceptance or rejection is likely is 1·4–6·5 per cent.

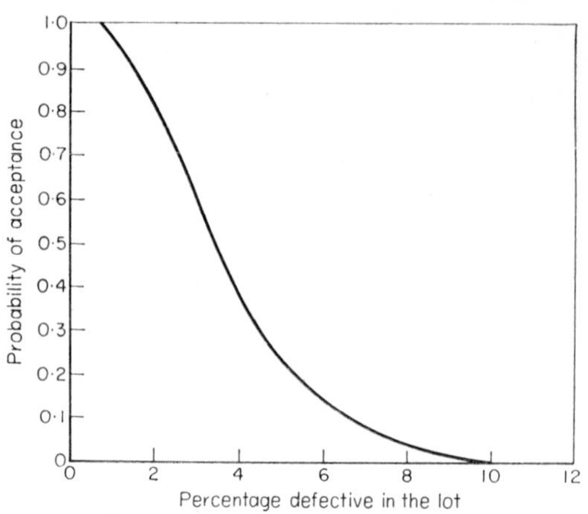

FIGURE 6.3 **Operating characteristic for a sample size of 80 and an acceptance number of 2**

Producer's Risk and Consumer's Risk

Attribute sampling is often used to decide whether or not goods made by a producer for supply to a consumer have a good enough quality to be accepted or whether they are so bad that they must be rejected. The producer and consumer must first agree upon the required attributes of the product and the methods of test or inspection. It is then usual for them to agree on a percentage of defective items which divide acceptable from rejectable lots. For example, they might agree that all lots containing 1 per cent or less defectives are acceptable and lots containing more than 1 per cent are rejectable.

The only way of determining exactly whether or not a particular lot meets the 1 per cent criterion is to inspect every item in the lot, continuing until more than 1 per cent of defectives have been found, and, of course, the inspection must be carried out with perfect efficiency.

Very often it is too expensive to carry out a 100 per cent inspection of this kind, covering all the defined attributes and using very precise inspection and test methods. The producer and consumer therefore agree to base their sentencing on sampling inspection. Where the agreed defective level is 1 per cent one common pair of sample size and acceptance number is 80 and 2 respectively. The operating characteristic of this pair has been given in Figure 6.3.

Because sampling cannot determine exactly whether or not any lot is better or worse than the agreed defective level the producer takes a certain risk that he will have good lots (better than the agreed level) rejected and the consumer takes a risk that he will accept bad lots (worse than the agreed level). From the operating characteristic of Figure 6.3 the producer's risk and the consumer's risk for this particular example can be seen. A lot that is 1 per cent defective, i. e. just acceptable, has a probability of 0·95 of being accepted and a probability of only 0·05 of being rejected. Lots of a quality better than the agreed level have an even higher probability of being accepted—a lot $\frac{1}{2}$ per cent defective has a probability of better than 0·99 of being accepted. For this particular example, the producer's risk of having a good lot rejected is quite small.

For the consumer the situation is different. A lot that is 1·1 per cent defective should be rejected. However the probability of such a lot being rejected is only 0·06 and the probability of its being accepted—the wrong decision—is 0·94. Even for a lot that is 2 per cent defective, twice as bad as the agreed defective level, the probability of making the correct decision and rejecting is only 0·2, whereas the probability of the wrong decision is 0·8. It is clear that this particular plan has a high risk for the consumer.

In summary, using an acceptance number of 2 and a sample size of 80 to measure whether or not lots are better or worse than 1 per cent defective is good for the producer but bad for the consumer.

Another example will now be considered, where the agreed quality level is 6·5 per cent defective, i.e. a much poorer quality than for the first example. However the producer and consumer could agree to use exactly the same sample size and acceptance number as before, 80 and 2 respectively, for judging the quality. From the operating characteristic of Figure 6.3 the producer submitting a lot which is just as good as the agreed level, 6.5 per cent defective, and which should therefore be accepted has, in fact, a 0·90 probability of having the lot rejected. The percentage defective has to be about half the agreed level before the producer has an even chance of getting a lot accepted. The producer's risk of having good lots rejected is therefore high. On the other hand the consumer's risk of accepting a bad lot is low. If the per cent defective is 6·6 per cent the chance of making the wrong decision and accepting is less than 0·1. Using a sample size of 80 and an acceptance number of 2 to measure whether or not lots are better or worse than 6·5 per cent defective is good for the consumer and bad for the producer.

It is sometimes said that the producer's risk and the consumer's risk added together give unity. This is not true as the producer and consumer cannot simultaneously be at risk: if the lot quality is as good or better than the agreed standard the consumer has no risk; if the quality is worse than the standard the producer has no risk (a bad lot cannot be *wrongly* rejected). However, the producer's risk at the

Table 6.1

BS 9001—Master Table for Single Sampling Plans for Normal Inspection

Sample size code letter	Sample size	Acceptable quality levels (normal inspection)																									
		0·010	0·015	0·025	0·040	0·065	0·10	0·15	0·25	0·40	0·65	1·0	1·5	2·5	4·0	6·5	10	15	25	40	65	100	150	250	400	650	1000
		Ac Re	Ac Re	Ac Re	Ac Re	Ac Re	Ac Re	Ac Re	Ac Re	Ac Re	Ac Re	Ac Re	Ac Re	Ac Re	Ac Re	Ac Re	Ac Re	Ac Re	Ac Re	Ac Re	Ac Re	Ac Re	Ac Re	Ac Re	Ac Re	Ac Re	Ac Re
A	2	⇩	⇩	⇩	⇩	⇩	⇩	⇩	⇩	⇩	⇩	⇩	⇩	⇩	⇩	0 1	⇩	⇩	1 2	2 3	3 4	5 6	7 8	10 11	14 15	21 22	30 31
B	3	⇩	⇩	⇩	⇩	⇩	⇩	⇩	⇩	⇩	⇩	⇩	⇩	⇩	0 1	⇧	⇩	1 2	2 3	3 4	5 6	7 8	10 11	14 15	21 22	30 31	44 45
C	5	⇩	⇩	⇩	⇩	⇩	⇩	⇩	⇩	⇩	⇩	⇩	⇩	0 1	⇧	⇩	1 2	2 3	3 4	5 6	7 8	10 11	14 15	21 22	30 31	44 45	⇧
D	8	⇩	⇩	⇩	⇩	⇩	⇩	⇩	⇩	⇩	⇩	⇩	0 1	⇧	⇩	1 2	2 3	3 4	5 6	7 8	10 11	14 15	21 22	30 31	44 45	⇧	⇧
E	13	⇩	⇩	⇩	⇩	⇩	⇩	⇩	⇩	⇩	⇩	0 1	⇧	⇩	1 2	2 3	3 4	5 6	7 8	10 11	14 15	21 22	30 31	44 45	⇧	⇧	⇧
F	20	⇩	⇩	⇩	⇩	⇩	⇩	⇩	⇩	⇩	0 1	⇧	⇩	1 2	2 3	3 4	5 6	7 8	10 11	14 15	21 22	⇧	⇧	⇧	⇧	⇧	⇧
G	32	⇩	⇩	⇩	⇩	⇩	⇩	⇩	⇩	0 1	⇧	⇩	1 2	2 3	3 4	5 6	7 8	10 11	14 15	21 22	⇧	⇧	⇧	⇧	⇧	⇧	⇧
H	50	⇩	⇩	⇩	⇩	⇩	⇩	⇩	0 1	⇧	⇩	1 2	2 3	3 4	5 6	7 8	10 11	14 15	21 22	⇧	⇧	⇧	⇧	⇧	⇧	⇧	⇧
J	80	⇩	⇩	⇩	⇩	⇩	⇩	0 1	⇧	⇩	1 2	2 3	3 4	5 6	7 8	10 11	14 15	21 22	⇧	⇧	⇧	⇧	⇧	⇧	⇧	⇧	⇧
K	125	⇩	⇩	⇩	⇩	⇩	0 1	⇧	⇩	1 2	2 3	3 4	5 6	7 8	10 11	14 15	21 22	⇧	⇧	⇧	⇧	⇧	⇧	⇧	⇧	⇧	⇧
L	200	⇩	⇩	⇩	⇩	0 1	⇧	⇩	1 2	2 3	3 4	5 6	7 8	10 11	14 15	21 22	⇧	⇧	⇧	⇧	⇧	⇧	⇧	⇧	⇧	⇧	⇧
M	315	⇩	⇩	⇩	0 1	⇧	⇩	1 2	2 3	3 4	5 6	7 8	10 11	14 15	21 22	⇧	⇧	⇧	⇧	⇧	⇧	⇧	⇧	⇧	⇧	⇧	⇧
N	500	⇩	⇩	0 1	⇧	⇩	1 2	2 3	3 4	5 6	7 8	10 11	14 15	21 22	⇧	⇧	⇧	⇧	⇧	⇧	⇧	⇧	⇧	⇧	⇧	⇧	⇧
P	800	⇩	0 1	⇧	⇩	1 2	2 3	3 4	5 6	7 8	10 11	14 15	21 22	⇧	⇧	⇧	⇧	⇧	⇧	⇧	⇧	⇧	⇧	⇧	⇧	⇧	⇧
Q	1250	0 1	⇧	⇩	1 2	2 3	3 4	5 6	7 8	10 11	14 15	21 22	⇧	⇧	⇧	⇧	⇧	⇧	⇧	⇧	⇧	⇧	⇧	⇧	⇧	⇧	⇧
R	2000	⇧	⇧	1 2	2 3	3 4	5 6	7 8	10 11	14 15	21 22	⇧	⇧	⇧	⇧	⇧	⇧	⇧	⇧	⇧	⇧	⇧	⇧	⇧	⇧	⇧	⇧

⇩ = Use first sampling plan below arrow. If sample size equals, or exceeds, lot or batch size, do 100 percent inspection

⇧ = Use first sampling plan above arrow

Ac = Acceptance number

agreed defective level and the consumer's risk at just worse than the agreed level add up to unity.

The examples have shown that exactly the same sample size and acceptance number can be used to judge two defective levels differing by 6·5 times, but in one case the consumer's risk was high and in the other the producer's risk was high.

AQL and LTPD

Where acceptance or rejection of lots is to be decided by sampling inspection two names are used for the agreed defective level. These are AQL, acceptable quality level, and LTPD, lot tolerance per cent defective. AQL is used when the sampling plan to be applied has a low producer's risk: often this is about 0·05 for a lot of a quality just equal to the AQL. In the examples discussed above the agreed standard of 1 per cent defective would be called a 1 per cent AQL, because the sampling plan used (sample size 80, acceptance number 2) had a low producer's risk.

Where the sampling plan has a low consumer's risk, often 0·10, the agreed defective level is called the LTPD. In the examples discussed above the agreed level of 6·5 per cent defective would be called a 6·5 per cent LTPD, because for this per cent defective the sampling plan of sample size 80 and acceptance number 2 has a low consumer's risk.

It is usually much more expensive to assure a given per cent defective by the LTPD method than by the AQL. In the examples discussed above the same sample size and acceptance number (and therefore the same cost of inspection) were used for an AQL of 1 per cent and an LTPD of 6·5 per cent. If an acceptance number of 2 is used an AQL of 6·5 per cent can be measured with a sample size of only 13, instead of the 80 needed for an LTPD of 6·5 per cent. Similarly, if an acceptance number of 2 is used the sample size has to be 533 to measure a 1 per cent LTPD, compared with 80 for the 1 per cent AQL.

BS 9001 AND MIL-STD-19500

The most widely used AQL sampling table was devised by a joint UK, USA and Canadian group and was issued as defence specifications DEF 131A in the UK and MIL-STD-105D in the USA. It has subsequently been issued as a British standard for general use, BS 9001. It is 66 pages long and one of these pages giving the most basic table of the plan is reproduced in Table 6.1.

Table 6.1 indicates various sample sizes and acceptance numbers that can be used to check different AQLs. Taking 1 per cent AQL as an example, this can be checked with a sample of 13 and an acceptance number of zero, or with a sample size of 1,250 and an acceptance number of 21. In each case, because this is an AQL table, the producer's risk of having a good lot rejected is held to a low value (between 0·01 and 0·12), but the consumer's risk of accepting a bad lot decreases progressively as the sample size is increased. The operating characteristics included in BS 9001 for a 1 per cent AQL show that the sampling plan with a sample size of 13 has a greater than 0·45 probability of accepting a lot that is 5 per cent defective. For the sample size of 80 this probability is reduced to 0·30 and for the sample size of 1,250 the probability is negligible.

An LTPD sampling table is included in the USA specification for semiconductor devices MIL-S-19500C and Table 6.2 is based on this.

Table 6.2 indicates the various sample sizes and acceptance numbers that can be used to check different LTPDs. Taking 1 per cent LTPD as an example this can be checked with a sample of 231 and an acceptance number of zero, or with a sample of 390 and an acceptance number of 1 or with the various other samples up to a sample size of 1,421 and an acceptance number of 9. In each case, because this is an LTPD table, the consumer's risk of accepting a bad lot is held to a low value (0·10), but the producer's risk of having a good lot rejected falls progressively as the sample size is increased. Figures included in MIL-S-19500 show that for a 1 per cent LTPD and a sample of 231 the lot can contain no more than 0·02 per cent defectives to have a high (0·95) probability of acceptance. For the sample size of 1,421 the lot has a 0·95 probability of acceptance if it is 0·38 per cent defective.

With an AQL sampling plan the producer's risk is held at a low level and the consumer's risk decreases as larger sample sizes are used; with an LTPD sampling plan the consumer's risk is held at a low level and the producer's risk decreases as larger sample sizes are used.

TESTING BY THE PRODUCER OR THE CONSUMER

In defining the methods to be used in accepting or rejecting lots by sampling inspection the producer or consumer must agree more than the required attributes, the methods of test, the AQL or the LTPD and the sampling plan. They must also decide who is to do the testing: the producer or the consumer. In practice, of course, whoever does the testing first, the other will often check the result by his own testing. There are basically four systems: (i) AQL testing by the consumer; (ii) AQL testing by the producer; (iii) LTPD testing by the

TABLE 6.2

Minimum Size of Sample to Assure with 90 per cent Confidence a Per Cent Defective no greater than the LTPD Specified

LTPD%	20	15	10	7	5	3	2	1·5	1	0·7	0·5	0·3	0·2	0·15	0·1
Acceptance No.	Minimum Sample Size														
0	11	15	22	32	45	76	116	153	231	328	461	767	1,152	1,534	2,303
1	18	25	38	55	77	129	195	258	390	555	778	1,246	1,946	2,592	3,841
2	25	34	52	75	105	176	266	354	533	759	1,065	1,773	2,662	3,547	5,323
3	32	43	65	94	132	221	333	444	668	953	1,337	2,226	3,341	4,452	6,681
4	38	52	78	113	158	265	398	531	798	1,140	1,599	2,663	3,997	5,327	7,994
5	45	60	91	131	184	308	462	617	927	1,323	1,855	3,090	4,638	6,181	9,275
6	51	68	104	149	209	349	518	700	1,054	1,503	2,107	3,509	5,267	7,019	10,533
7	57	77	116	166	234	390	589	783	1,178	1,680	2,355	3,922	5,886	7,845	11,771
8	63	85	128	184	258	431	648	864	1,300	1,854	2,599	4,329	6,498	8,660	12,995
9	69	93	140	201	282	471	709	945	1,421	2,207	2,842	4,733	7,103	9,468	14,206

producer; (iv) LTPD testing by the consumer. These will be considered in turn.

The simplest category is the first, AQL testing by the consumer. If a 1 per cent AQL is agreed, for example, the producer is contractually required to supply lots that are no more than 1 per cent defective (but see page 103 below). The consumer checks this by inspecting, using an AQL sampling plan. Because this is a low *producer's* risk plan it is unlikely that any lots the consumer rejects will be better than the agreed AQL, so the producer should have no grounds for complaint. The consumer can increase his own protection by using a large sample size and acceptance number, or reduce his costs by using a small sample. The consumer usually has no motive for rejecting good lots, so the producer's only reasons for checking rejections by his own re-inspection is if he doubts the competence of the consumer to carry out the inspection correctly.

There are obvious advantages in the testing being performed by the producer rather than the consumer and the second category, AQL testing by the producer, is often applied. However, this is more complicated than the first category. For a 1 per cent AQL the producer is required to supply lots that are no worse than 1 per cent defective and to check this by inspection using an AQL sampling plan. The producer has obvious motives for skimping the testing or even for supplying lots that have failed the testing, so the consumer may feel obliged from time to time to check the quality by his own re-inspection (alternatives are to require the producer to submit his test results for scrutiny, or even for the consumer to install a supervising inspector at the supplier's plant). The consumer should carry out his re-inspection using an AQL plan. This should ensure that he will only reject lots that are worse than the agreed AQL. However, it may well reject lots that the producer has quite honestly tested according to the agreement, because the producer's AQL testing can accept lots that *are* markedly worse than the AQL, particularly if small sample sizes are used. The producer is commonly angered by such rejections and he will dispute them, using arguments such as "double jeopardy". One answer is for the consumer to require that the producer uses large sample sizes for the initial AQL testing. However, the consumer may not be willing to pay the price for this. The consumer should make clear before the contract is signed that the producer's prime responsibility is to supply lots with a per cent defective no worse than the AQL, and that the requirement for him to carry out specified AQL testing is secondary. If the consumer at his own cost carries out additional testing which shows that a lot is worse than the AQL, then it is rejectable, even if it has previously passed the producer's AQL testing. An alternative, but less satisfactory agreement, is for the consumer to reserve the right to reject lots only if his own re-inspection indicates that the producer has not correctly performed the required inspection. This will usually mean that the consumer can only reject lots that are several times worse than the AQL (see also series-lot testing, page 103 below).

The third alternative is LTPD testing by the producer. In principle this is a good system but in practice it has a number of difficulties. If a 1 per cent LTPD is specified the producer is required to supply lots that are no worse than 1 per cent defective and to check this using a sampling plan that has a low consumer's risk. Unfortunately this is difficult for the producer. The smallest sample size he can use (see Table 6.2) is 231 and with this the defective level has to be fifty times better than the LTPD (0·02 per cent defective) for the producer to have a high probability (0·95) of getting the lot accepted. Even with a large sample of 1,421, which will usually make testing very expensive, the lot defective level can be no higher than 0·38 per cent for there to be a 0·95 probability of acceptance. Because the majority of lots which fail the producer's own inspection will in fact be better than the LTPD, the producer has an obvious motive to supply lots which have failed the testing. The consumer has no good way of checking this by his own re-inspection. If he does LTPD testing with a low sample size he will reject many lots which are better than the LTPD and the producer's arguments of double jeopardy will now be quite valid. AQL testing with small sample sizes will usually pass all lots and reveal nothing. Only AQL testing with very large sample sizes will be both statistically sound and practically useful, but this is usually expensive. LTPD testing by the producer is probably only practicable where the consumer keeps a resident supervising inspector at the producer's plant and even then the cost will normally be high (see page 102 below).

The fourth alternative is LTPD testing by the consumer. This puts the producer in a very difficult position. He may agree to supply to a 1 per cent LTPD, which means that lots with a defective level no worse than 1 per cent should be acceptable. However, the producer knows that the consumer is using a sampling plan that will reject many lots that are better than 1 per cent defective. If the consumer chooses to use a small sample size, e.g. 231, the producer knows that lots that are far better than the LTPD can be rejected. The situation is ameliorated somewhat if the producer insists (at the contract stage) that the consumer uses a high sample size, but this is, of course, expensive.

In the writer's opinion, AQL testing is on the whole more satisfactory that LTPD testing. The latter only works well when lot sizes are very large so that sample sizes can be large and yet be only a small fraction of the lot size. Where sample sizes are limited by cost it is better to use AQL testing. If a consumer needs lots that are no worse than 1 per cent defective, and yet is only able to pay for testing a sample of 80 from each lot, he does better to specify a 1 per cent AQL than a 6·5 per cent LTPD. Both will accept lots with an acceptance number of 2, but the former tells the producer that 1 per cent defective is required whereas the latter only required 6·5 per cent defective.

In summary, the best agreement between producer and consumer for sampling inspection will often be:

(i) for consumer and producer to agree a particular percentage defective;

(ii) for the producer to agree to supply each lot with a percentage defective no worse than the particular level agreed;

(iii) for the producer to use manufacturing methods and 100 per cent screening procedures compatible with (ii) (this is of paramount importance);

(iv) for the producer to agree to sample inspect each lot to the agreed percentage defective and an agreed inspection level (see page 101 below) using BS 9001, i.e. to use an AQL, low producer's risk, plan—he also agrees to apply the tightened inspection rules of BS 9001;

(v) for the producer to agree to supply the sample inspection results on each lot to the consumer;

(vi) for the producer to agree to take immediate and effective corrective action with regard to his manufacturing methods if the process average[1] is, or appears likely to go, worse than the agreed AQL.

(vii) for the consumer to have the right to inspect lots, at his own cost, and to reject each one for which his results indicate with high probability a per cent defective worse than the AQL—this means the consumer must use an AQL plan (BS 9001), not an LTPD plan, though he can reduce his consumer's risk by using as large a sample size as he is prepared to pay for;

(viii) for the producer to accept such rejections, even though his own sampling had previously accepted the lot (because his prime responsibility is to supply lots no worse than the AQL and the consumer's sampling had shown that for the rejected lot he had failed to do that);

(ix) for the producer to have no right to supply an item he knows to be defective, e.g. by supplying items discovered defective during the sampling test, or by adding defective items to very good lots to bring the defective level up to the AQL.

[1] See page 103 below for definition of process average.

The primary assumptions of the above scheme are that the producer has manufacturing methods that are fully capable of making a product with a per cent defective no worse than the AQL, and that sampling inspection is used as economically as possible to check that capability. All too often producers agree to AQLs that they are not fully capable of meeting (or to prices that are too low to allow them to meet the AQL and make a profit) and then rely on the sampling characteristics to get lots through which are two or three times worse than the AQL.

INSPECTION LEVELS AND LOT SIZES

It was noted above that when the producer was required to do the testing for AQL sampling, the consumer might require him to use samples no smaller than a given size. This was because, with AQL sampling, the producer's risk of wrongly having a lot rejected was more or less independent of the sample size and obviously the cost to him of testing was lower with small samples than with large. On the other hand the consumer's risk of accepting lots markedly worse than the AQL was decreased by inspecting large samples. In BS 9001 inspection levels are used to cover this point. There are seven different inspection levels: S1, S2, S3, S4, I, II, and III. Each of these, together with the lot size, fixes a sample size. Table 6.3, which is based on Table 1 of BS 9001 shows how this is done. For example, with a lot size of 5,000 the most stringent inspection level, III, requires a sample size of 315 and the least stringent, S1, a sample size of 5. With a smaller lot size, e.g. 500, inspection level III requires a sample size of 80 and inspection level S1 a sample size of only 3. It is apparent from Table 6.3 that the seven different, available inspection levels of BS 9001 give a very large range of sample sizes for a given lot size.

The cost of and the amount of information obtained by a particular inspection are independent of the lot size: it is the sample size that controls both. It costs no more to inspect a sample of 80 taken from a lot of 500 than a sample of the same size taken from a lot of 5,000. And the consumer's risk of accepting a lot more defective than the AQL is the same in both cases. However, the cost of the inspection *for each item released* is ten times as great for the former case as the latter. BS 9001 takes advantage of the lower unit cost of inspection for larger lot sizes to increase sample sizes. This means that the consumer's risk of accepting lots more defective than the AQL is lower for large lots than for small lots when BS 9001 is used. This is reasonable because the disadvantages of accepting a large lot of a particular item, which is worse than the AQL, are likely to be greater than those of accepting a small lot.

TABLE 6.3

BS 9001 Inspection Levels and Sample Sizes for Single Sampling

Lot Size	Special Inspection Levels				General Inspection Levels		
	S1	S2	S3	S4	I	II	III
2 to 8	2	2	2	2	2	2	3
9 to 15	2	2	2	2	2	3	5
16 to 25	2	2	3	3	3	5	8
26 to 50	2	3	3	5	5	8	13
51 to 90	3	3	5	5	5	13	20
91 to 150	3	3	5	8	8	20	32
151 to 280	3	5	8	13	13	32	50
281 to 500	3	5	8	13	20	50	80
501 to 1,200	5	5	13	20	32	80	125
1,201 to 3,200	5	8	13	32	50	125	200
3,201 to 10,000	5	8	20	32	80	200	315
10,001 to 35,000	5	8	20	50	125	315	500
35,001 to 150,000	8	13	32	80	200	500	800
150,001 to 500,000	8	13	32	80	315	800	1250
500,001 and over	8	13	50	125	500	1250	2000

Sample size

At the same time for a given inspection level BS 9001 requires sample sizes that are a smaller proportion of the lot as the lot size increases. This means that the cost of inspection per item released is smaller for large lots. In general, lot sizes play a major part in determining the practicability of sampling inspection. Acceptance inspection by sampling only becomes possible at all when the lot size is at least as great as the reciprocal of the AQL (e.g. a minimum lot size of 100 for a 1 per cent AQL, see page 110 below). When the lot size is ten times the reciprocal of the AQL the system works well. At lot sizes 100 or more times greater than the reciprocal of the AQL, the system works very efficiently, the cost of inspection per item released is small unless the unit cost of inspection is exceptionally great and high acceptance numbers can be used with a corresponding reduction in consumer's risk.

Of course, there are objections to big lot sizes, even where the production rate is high. Product must be held until the required lot size is accumulated and this increases inventory and storage costs. Also the problems associated with lot rejection are magnified by large lots. Usually, lot sizes consist of the production made in periods within the range of a few hours to one week.

ISOLATED LOT AND SERIES OF LOTS

Everything that has been written so far in this chapter has been essentially concerned with single, isolated lots whose acceptance or rejection is based entirely upon the results of inspection of a sample randomly taken from the lot. The terms AQL, LTPD, producer's risk and consumer's risk have been discussed in this context. When the required defective level is specified as an LTPD the isolated lot concept is usually assumed. However, when an AQL is specified there is often an assumption of a continuing series of lots, and acceptance or rejection of the current lot is not dependent only upon the results of the tests on the sample taken from it. Information is also utilized from the results of tests of previous samples. The definition of AQL used in BS 9001 is: "The AQL is the maximum per cent defective . . . that for purposes of sampling inspection, can be considered satisfactory as a process average." (Process average is the average per cent defective in lots submitted for original inspection and is usually estimated from the results of tests on samples drawn from the five most recent lots.) The term process average can only be applied to a series of lots and it has been shown above that an isolated lot can have a per cent defective much worse than the AQL and yet still have a good chance of being accepted. By working on a series of lots the aim of BS 9001 is to reject lots from a product line which, on average, is producing a defective level worse than the AQL.

The main device for doing this is the use of "tightened inspection". Tightened inspection is "instituted when 2 out of 5 consecutive lots . . . have been rejected on original inspection". If the process average is appreciably worse than the AQL the required two lots will soon be failed and tightened inspection will be introduced. It is clear that this will happen more quickly and with less margin above the AQL if a high inspection level rather than a low is in use.

When AQL inspection is being used on a series of lots it is greatly to the consumer's advantage to insist that the tightened inspection conditions of BS 9001 are applied. It markedly reduces the consumer's risk of accepting lots more defective than the AQL. For a series of lots the tightened-inspection device increases the advantage of AQL over LTPD testing because it gives much of the protection of the consumer associated with the latter and the lower cost of the former. The consumer may receive some lots that are worse than the AQL, but the process average should not be worse than the AQL.

SETTING THE AQL

The first part of this chapter has been concerned with the mathematical basis of sampling and the simple logic that governs its application. This section will be concerned with matters for which the quality engineer must exercise judgement and which can therefore cause more difficulty. When the attributes of the products and the methods of inspection or test are defined and the AQL and inspection level agreed, performance of the inspection is a mechanical process. It is in the setting of the AQL and the inspection level that judgement is required. The methods to be used will depend upon the circumstances, examples of which are listed below:

(i) a mass-produced component produced "in house" for use in one specific sub-assembly;
(ii) a mass-produced component made for one consumer for use in one specific sub-assembly;
(iii) a mass-produced component bought by many consumers for use in many applications;
(iv) a sub-assembly;
(v) an equipment to be offered for sale.

The first example, a mass-produced component produced in house for use in a specific sub-assembly, is in principle the simplest. It can be assumed that the proportion of defective components existing in the sub-assembly must be brought down to a particular level. This level is achieved by (i) controlling the per cent defective of the components used and (ii) by inspection, test and re-work of the sub-assembly. The cost of the two parts is adjusted by changing the component AQL to give the minimum total cost. If the AQL is tightened, the cost of achieving it may increase (a more expensive manufacturing process may have to be used, 100 per cent screening may be needed, etc.). On the other hand the cost of inspection, test and re-work of the sub-assembly should be reduced. Whether or not to introduce 100 per cent screening[1] consider a number of components N of which a proportion P is defective. Let I be the cost of inspecting one component and A the cost of finding and re-working one defective component in the sub-assembly. If 100 per cent component inspection is carried out it is assumed (although this cannot be strictly correct) that $A = 0$, and the cost is simply the cost of screening, i.e. NI.

If component inspection is not performed the cost is the cost of re-work, i.e. PNA.

[1] See Duran, *Quality Control Handbook*, 2nd edition (McGraw-Hill).

It is therefore cheaper to screen if:

NI is less than PNA, i.e. if I/A is less than P.

$p^1 = I/A$ is the proportion defective at which the advantage just changes from component screening to sub-assembly test and re-work. Sampling could be introduced on the component using a plan that has an even chance of accepting lots that are p^1 defective. Rejected lots would be 100 per cent screened and accepted lots would be used in sub-assembly manufacture without screening.

In practice this system of calculating the AQL is rarely adopted because of the difficulty of estimating the costs I and A. The case is also artificial because it is often cheaper to improve the component-manufacturing process than to introduce 100 per cent screening.

A common variation of the above situation is where serious problems are occurring in the sub-assembly manufacture because of the proportion of defective components. AQL sampling is introduced as a means of controlling this. The AQL is then decided by measuring the current per cent defective of the component—it might be 7 per cent. Immediately applicable corrective action if energetically and conscientiously applied could reduce this by a factor of 5. An AQL of 1·5 per cent might then be applicable. Reducing the per cent defective from 7 to 1·5 per cent will certainly greatly ease the problems in the sub-assembly manufacture. The 1·5 per cent AQL might still be worse than that to give the cost optimum, but immediate application of a tighter AQL would shut off the supply of the component and stop the manufacture of the sub-assembly.

Another common variation is where 100 per cent screening of the component has been applied, but the manufacturing process has been improved and the proportion of defective components eliminated by the screen is now small. The question is asked: can the 100 per cent screen be replaced by cheaper sampling inspection and if so what should the AQL be? In principle the question can be answered by a careful examination of the costs. In practice, the second part of the question is easily answered. The AQL should be the per cent defective as measured by the 100 per cent screen. A tighter AQL will cause lot rejections and reimpose the 100 per cent screen: a looser AQL implies that there would be a cost advantage in letting the component-manufacturing process deteriorate and this is unlikely to be true. Is the AQL, determined in that way, acceptable so that the 100 per cent screen can be eliminated? If an extra stage of testing of the sub-assembly will then be required the answer is almost certainly no. If however the AQL is comparable to the defective level of other components used in the sub-asssmbly, or of defects introduced by the assembly process, then it is very likely that the 100 per cent screen can be replaced by

AQL sampling—particularly if elimination of the screen gives an important cost saving.

The second example—a mass-produced component made for one customer for use in one specific sub-assembly—would seem technically the same as the first. The ideal AQL should be that which minimizes the total cost of the component maker and his customer and the price of the component should be set fairly to take account of this. In practice it will be more difficult to achieve this optimum with two parties rather than one involved. The consumer is probably advised to devote his efforts to getting the supplier's agreement to a "reasonable" AQL (see below) and then ensuring that he meets it.

In the third example—a mass-produced component bought by many consumers for many applications—it is virtually impossible to calculate the optimum AQL to minimize the total costs of all of the parties involved. The AQL is then set arbitrarily at a "reasonable" value. This is normally a 1 per cent AQL or an AQL near to this, say 0·4 to 4 per cent. There are good reasons for this. A component that is 10 per cent defective will cause obvious problems in most applications. Also, simple corrective action will usually reduce a per cent defective as bad as this. So, a 10 per cent AQL is not usual for a component. On the other hand to achieve a 0·1 per cent defective level is normally quite difficult for the supplier. And most customers will be unable to determine whether or not it is being achieved. Incoming inspection would have to be done with sample sizes of 500 or more (to have a tolerable consumer's risk) or, alternatively, assembly-line defect information would have to be collected and analysed with great care. Even for simple components where achievement of a per cent defective of 0·1 per cent or better is quite practicable, application of lot sampling with a tight AQL is not usually applied. The supplier will simply rely on process controls and will not do formal lot sampling to check the per cent defective. For these reasons 0·1 per cent AQLs are not common for components. In short, an AQL near to 1 per cent can usually be set for a component with confidence. It may not be the optimum but nothing terrible is likely to happen if it is applied. In some circumstances, experience will later show that costs can be optimized by tightening the AQL, or relying on process control.

The fourth example is a sub-assembly. A digression into categorization of defects is needed before this can be discussed. In BS 9001 defects are categorized as critical, major and minor:

> *Critical defect.* A critical defect is a defect that judgement and experience indicate is likely to result in hazardous or unsafe conditions for individuals using, maintaining, or depending upon the product; or a defect that judgement and experience indicate is likely to prevent performance of the tactical function of a major end item such as a ship, aircraft, tank, missile or space vehicle.

Major defect. A major defect is a defect, other than critical, that is likely to result in failure, or to reduce materially the usability of the unit of product for its intended purpose.
Minor defect. A minor defect is a defect that is not likely to reduce materially the usability of the unit of product for its intended purpose, or is a departure from established standards having little bearing on the effective use or operation of the unit.

It would seem reasonable that critical defects would be very severely controlled by applying an extremely tight AQL, major defects would have a moderately tight AQL and minor defects a fairly loose AQL. Although this is not always realized by workers in quality control, the above definitions of defects are not properly applicable to components and sub-assemblies. Of course, a particular defect in a sub-assembly may in the end "prevent performance of the technical function of a major end item such as a ship", but this does not mean that it must necessarily be classified as critical at the stage of sub-assembly test. It should be classed as critical at this stage only if there is a reasonable probability that it will not be discovered at other later stages of test on the assembly or on the major end item itself.

In practice there is another important classification of defects:

(i) defects that produce an immediately observable effect on the functional performance of the item;

(ii) defects that do not produce an immediately observable effect on the functional performance of the item.

Defects in the first category can usually be found with great efficiency by testing the performance of the item. For example, a sub-assembly such as the amplifier of a record player which passes a simple performance test will be known to be free of a large number of possible defects. None of the scores of soldered joints are open circuit: none of the many components are seriously defective or wrongly placed in the circuit. The proportion of defects of that category can therefore be brought to an extremely low level by process-control testing, re-work and re-testing—and it is, of course, necessary that it shall. In principle this means that the achievement of a satisfactory defect level could be checked by lot-sampling of the sub-assemblies for such defects using a tight AQL. In practice lot-sampling with tight AQLs presents difficulties. Even a 1 per cent AQL may not be practicable for a sub-assembly which may not be made in large quantities. The effectiveness of the 100 per cent testing and re-work in eliminating functional defects may therefore be checked by quality auditing (see page 111 below) rather than by sampling acceptance.

Defects of the other kind—those that do not produce an immediately observable effect on the functional performance—cannot be eliminated efficiently by test and re-work. The question can be asked: if they do not affect the immediate performance why are they categorized as defects? There are several reasons. First, they may affect the future performance, i. e. they are defects reducing the reliability or durability of the item. Secondly, they may concern the appearance of the item—and this can be of major importance to the customer, particularly with consumer products. Thirdly, the customer, for his own reasons, sensible or not, may require control of these defects (one of the non-sensible reasons is where the customer's inspectors are particularly good at finding defects of a particular kind and another is where the customer subjectively feels a particular defect has a more important effect on reliability than in fact it does). Examples of defects of this kind are: scratches on the cabinet of a television set, corrosion on metal parts, and solder joints which do not conform to workmanship standards even though they are not functionally open-circuit.

Defects of this kind must be found individually. There is usually no test that can be done that in one application will find a large number of such defects. Fortunately, because they do not affect functional performance it is usually unnecessary to reduce the proportion of such defects to an extremely low level. Sampling lot acceptance procedures can then be very useful. For example, field-use results might show that solder joints visually defective in a particular way had only a trivial effect on the reliability of an equipment provided no more than 0·4 per cent of the joints were defective in this way. At proportions less than this the specified equipment reliability was achieved and the main factor involved was the reliability of particular components used. With no lot sampling the proportion of visually defective solder joints might be 1 or 2 per cent because attention was concentrated on immediate functional performance. Inspecting a sample of 200 solder joints on each lot of sub-assemblies and rejecting if more than two defects were found, would be a practical way of assuring the 0·4 per cent AQL.[1] An important point is that for defects of this kind the sampling is based upon the possible defect sites rather than upon the item under inspection. One sub-assembly of the equipment might contain 1,000 solder joints, another might contain 5,000. In each the proportion of defective joints would be controlled to 0·4 per cent. The control would *not* be to ensure that each sub-assembly contained say no more than ten defective joints.

[1] Large pieces of electronic equipment may contain hundreds of thousands of solder joints and it is quite practicable to inspect a sample of 2,000 joints from such an equipment. This therefore gives an example where it is economically possible and useful to apply a very tight AQL, e.g. 0·025 per cent.

In summary, for the fourth example, a sub-assembly, defects causing loss of functional performance are usually controlled by 100 per cent testing and monitored by quality auditing. Defects of the other kind can be assured by lot acceptance and the AQLs, referred to the possible defect sites, are usually similar to those for components.

For the last example, an equipment to be offered for sale is similar in many respects to a sub-assembly, except that the acceptance procedure may be contractually agreed with the customer. Functional performance is usually tested 100 per cent, and any deficiencies cause re-work and further 100 per cent testing. For small equipments made in a continuing series quality auditing (see below) of functional performance is extremely desirable but lot acceptance is likely to be impracticable. For large, one-off equipments this will almost certainly be the case. Non-functional defects can be assured by acceptance sampling related to the number of possible defect sites.

One case where the functional performance of a major equipment or system can be assured by acceptance sampling is where some particular failure rate is acceptable. An example of this is in "lost calls" through a new telephone exchange. The requirement may be for no more than a specified proportion of lost calls and the acceptance procedure might require some thousands of calls to be put through the exchange of which no more than a certain acceptance number can be lost.

SETTING THE INSPECTION LEVEL

In addition to needing to use judgement in setting the AQL for a sampling inspection the quality engineer also needs to use judgement in setting the inspection level. The latter determines how large a sample must be taken from a lot of a particular size. In BS 9001 the seven different inspection levels combine a wide range of sample sizes for the same lot size. In the example discussed above for a lot size of 5,000 the largest sample was 315 and the smallest 5. How is the decision taken to use a particular inspection level? BS 9001 itself says, "Unless otherwise specified inspection level II will be used," but there are many circumstances in which other inspection levels are appropriate. The two main principles are that the cost of the sampling inspection is reduced by using a low inspection level and that the consumer's risk of accepting lots which contain more defects than the AQL is reduced by using a high inspection level. (With an AQL sampling plan, as noted above, the inspection level does not have a major effect on the producer's risk of having lots rejected which are better than the

AQL). The correct inspection level is determined by balancing these two opposing factors. In doing this there are a number of guides. The first is that there is a direct relationship between AQL and minimum sample size. The smallest sample that can be used to check a particular AQL is that for which an acceptance number of zero is used. The consumer's risk is particularly high for an acceptance number of zero so, if cost will allow it, it is better to use an acceptance number of 1. The corresponding values of AQL and sample size which then result are given in Table 6.4.

TABLE 6.4

Sample Sizes Related to AQL for Acceptance Numbers of 0 and 1 (BS 9001 Single Sampling, Normal Inspection)

AQL%	Sample Size for Acceptance Numbers	
	0	1
0·10	125	500
0·15	80	315
0·25	50	200
0·40	32	125
0·65	20	80
1·0	13	50
1·5	8	32
2·5	5	20
4·0	3	13
6·5	2	8

If an AQL of 0·10 per cent is specified then the minimum sample size is 125 and if possible 500 should be used. Depending upon the range of lot sizes, the inspection level must be set to give sample sizes at least as large as this. Once a 0·10 per cent AQL is set the cost of inspection cannot be lower than that required by these sample sizes. If a higher AQL is set, e.g. 1 per cent, then much smaller sample sizes can be used: 13 or 50 for acceptance numbers of zero and one respectively. The cost of sampling inspection can be lower.

The preceding paragraph discusses the minimum cost of inspecting for particular AQLs. However, the consumer's risk will be much better if higher acceptance numbers, e.g. 3 or 5, are used. For a 1 per cent AQL this increases the sample size to 125 or 200 with a corre-ponding increase in cost of inspection. The lot per cent defective that has an even chance of being accepted by the various 1 per cent AQL sampling plans with acceptance numbers of 0, 1, 3 and 5 are given in Table 6.5.

TABLE 6.5

Lot Per cent Defectives Having Even Chance of Acceptance for 1% AQL Sampling Plans

Sample Size	Acceptance Number	Lot % defective for 0·5 Probability of Acceptance
13	0	5·19
50	1	3·33
125	3	2·94
200	5	2·84

This shows that with the smallest sample size the consumer has a high chance of accepting lots that are more than 5 per cent defective. With a larger sample size the consumer has protection at a lower per cent defective.

Except where the cost of inspection is very low or the lot size very large, it is not usually economical to use sampling plans with high acceptance numbers (see page 102 above).

ACCEPTANCE INSPECTION, QUALITY AUDITING AND MANAGEMENT ACTION

Earlier in this chapter the essential features of acceptance inspection by sampling were described. A sample of product was randomly taken from a lot of the product. The sample was inspected while the lot was held. If the sample was found to contain no more defectives than the acceptance number the lot was released to the customer. This process exercises a considerable degree of control on the quality of the product. The group carrying out such an acceptance inspection as a last stage before dispatching to the customer can be said to be "responsible" for the outgoing quality. Their control will not be perfect, because they may not be able to test or inspect all the required attributes of the product, the test and inspection methods they use will not be completely efficient and their sampling plans will have a finite consumer's risk, but none the less they should be in a good position to prevent most defective lots going to the customer.

Sampling inspection can be used for a different purpose: not to stop defective product going to the customer, but to give the management of the producer a measure of the product defective level going to the customer. Sampling inspection used for this purpose is called "product-quality auditing". There are a number of differences between acceptance inspection and quality auditing. The actual process of inspection is similar but in quality auditing the lot is not held while the inspection is carried out, and the product may well go to the customer before the inspection is complete. The most important difference arises from this: the group carrying out a product-quality audit is *not* responsible for the quality of the outgoing product. Their job is simply to measure the defective level and report it clearly to management. Responsibility for outgoing quality rests with some other group, e.g. a final test and inspection group or the production department. The quality-audit group measures the effectiveness of groups working earlier in the production cycle. If the latter are ineffective and the outgoing product does not conform to its requirements, management action must be directed at improvement at these earlier stages of the production cycle; it should not try to use the audit as a further screen.

Because quality auditing does not delay shipment of product, nor control outgoing quality, it is not governed by the relationships between AQL, inspection level and lot size that apply to acceptance inspection. In an earlier section we saw that to carry out acceptance inspection to a 0·1 per cent AQL required a minimum sample of 125 and that it would be better to use a sample of 500 or more. The cost of such sampling inspection can be expected to be a significant fraction of the cost of each unit of product unless the lot sizes are large, say 10,000 or more. For a quality audit these restrictions do not apply. Assume the product requiring the 0·1 per cent AQL was made at a rate of 1,000 per day. For an audit it would be quite reasonable to take a sample of 50 each day. If the defective level was at the AQL, on average one defect would be found every twenty days. However, if the product was twice as bad as this, defectives would be found every ten days. Within a month management would know that some corrective action was needed to the process and provided this was taken quickly it would be quite likely that the customer (or customers) would not notice the deterioration. A more serious deterioration, say to 1 per cent defective, would be indicated within a few days and a gross deterioration might be indicated by the first sample. In this latter case, e.g. if one sample contained four or five defectives, the audit might serve as an acceptance inspection and prevent dispatch of defective product. However, it must be emphasized that the purpose of an audit is to tell management about the quality of its outgoing product. It is only useful if management then sees that prompt and effective corrective action is applied to previous processes and inspections as soon as the audit reveals trouble.

To some extent the differences between sampling-acceptance inspections and quality audits are illusory. Properly carried out, sampling-acceptance inspection becomes very similar to quality auditing. Consider a product submitted to sampling-acceptance inspection to a 1 per cent AQL using a sample size of 80 and an acceptance number of 2. The operating characteristic (Figure 6.3, page 92) shows that, while lots that are 1 per cent defective are submitted, most will be accepted and about 1 in 20 will be rejected. However, if the quality deteriorates to 3 per cent defective nearly half of the lots will be rejected, very soon "2 out of 5 consecutive lots" will be rejected, and tightened inspection will be imposed. If the per cent defective remains at 3 per cent more than two-thirds of the lots will then be rejected. The whole situation then insistently demands the kind of corrective action, initiated by management, that should be the consequence of poor results given by a quality audit.

On the other hand, if the product is particularly good "reduced inspection" (see BS 9001) is earned after 10 consecutive lots have been accepted and the total number of defectives found in the 10 samples is less than a specified number (in fact 4 for our example). This reduced sampling level then becomes very inefficient in rejecting individual lots that are worse than the AQL and becomes in effect a quality audit giving management information.

In summary an acceptance inspection works effectively while the product-defective level is near to the AQL (in our 1 per cent AQL example say in the range 0·5 to 2 per cent) but outside that range it becomes little different from a quality audit. All too often acceptance inspection is looked upon as a static system which can be left to run. However, the aim should always be to improve control to the level where acceptance can be replaced by audit. And the situation should never be allowed to continue where a high proportion of lots are rejected (this is only possible if the tightened-inspection rules are ignored) because this inevitably means that the *accepted* lots will be worse than the AQL, and is, of course, very expensive in re-work and re-inspection.

Perhaps the most important aspect of sampling inspection either for acceptance or audit is that, when properly carried out, it does force management attention in a way that 100 per cent inspection does not. With the latter, product can be submitted to test and inspection, and large numbers of defects can be found and failures occur. The product is then re-worked and goes to the customer either without check or after check of the re-worked defects. No data analysis is made and no reports go to management. This system can be applied indefinitely;

all it requires is a good number of inspectors, testers and re-work operators. The product going to the customer may not be very good, but it is usually good enough to get by. The system requires little or no attention from higher management except occasional pressure on the chief inspector to be "tougher" when customer complaints are received. It is a cosy system but very expensive and only marginally effective.

Sampling inspection on the other hand does demand attention from higher management. Deterioration of quality with an acceptance-inspection system rapidly causes a dramatic situation as rejected lots accumulate and output drops. Corrective action must then be applied and this involves management. With a quality-auditing system the only reason for doing the auditing is to get management attention and corrective action and a quality department expert enough to do product-quality auditing is usually expert enough to get the required action.

Product-quality auditing is at the same time the most effective and the most difficult system of inspection. It is difficult, because it adds a measurable amount of cost (though a small amount) and itself achieves nothing: it does not enable re-work of defective product or prevent bad product going to the customer or cut costs or speed production. It is also difficult because it reveals clearly to management problems that the latter must then cause to be solved. And very often management has enough problems with costs and sales and prefers to remain in ignorance of conformance problems. But solution of the conformance problems usually gives a major contribution to solution of the cost and sales problems.

7 *Supplier Quality Control*

For most manufacturing organizations purchasing and sub-contracting are a major part of the business. With the increasing specialization of modern manufacturing, it is rare for a unit to buy natural materials and itself carry through all the processes required to make a product for the ultimate user. In some industries virtually all the components and sub-assemblies are purchased and the organization completing the product for the ultimate user is concerned only with design, marketing and final assembly and test. Controlling the quality of purchased supplies and sub-contracted work is therefore a major aspect of quality control.

In an ideal world the engineering department would obtain samples of the needed components or materials, would try them in prototypes of the items to be manufactured and, finding them satisfactory, would authorize Purchasing to buy production quantities. These would arrive on schedule, would be identical to the samples and would be used by Manufacturing without problem, the final product having the required performance. In the real world the situation is, of course, very different.

PURCHASING SPECIFICATIONS

In supplier quality control the emphasis must be upon conformance. Without this no control is possible. The simplest kind of conformance would be the requirement that production quantities of the purchased item should be exactly like the samples. This is usually an impossible requirement and no supplier would accept a contract written in that way. The required conformance will therefore be to written specifications, prepared either by the supplier, the purchaser or some independent body such as a national standards organization. These specifications will define the essential features of the product including one or more of the six types of specification discussed in Chapter 1. Supplier quality control starts with the purchasing specifications, and the importance of good specifications cannot be over-emphasized. If the specifications are prepared by the user he must be sure that they include all the requirements needed. He must also make sure that the supplier completely understands the specifications. If the specifications are prepared by the supplier (possibly for one of his standard range) the user must still be sure that they cover all his requirements and in addition he must be sure that *he* completely understands the specifications. Later in this chapter electronic components will be used as an example for a more detailed consideration of purchasing specifications. At this stage it will merely be stated that it is usually important to specify not only what the purchased items must be or must do, but also how this is to be checked by inspection or test. Responsibility for specifiying the purchased items (or ascertaining that a national specification covers the requirement correctly) rests with the technical function. Quality engineering will participate in the specification of the tests and inspections to be applied.

Accepting that the goods for purchasing are adequately specified it is then the responsibility of the purchasing department to buy products that conform exactly to the specified requirements. This statement is so important that it is worth repeating. Just as it is the responsibility of the manufacturing department to make products that conform to the requirements, it is the responsibility of the purchasing department to buy products that conform to the requirements. Obviously, the work of the purchasing department is easier if it ignores conformance and concentrates only upon negotiating low prices and early deliveries. Getting satisfactory results from suppliers is a team effort involving the purchasing, technical and quality departments, but to a large extent the primary responsibility rests with Purchasing. It should encourage and demand work from the other departments in accurate specification and effective quality control, recognizing that these will assist it in fulfilling its own responsibilities. General management should judge the purchasing department at least as much on its ability to buy products that do their job as on its cost-reduction and schedule activities.

An effective supplier quality-control programme is virtually impossible without good, working co-operation between the customer's purchasing, engineering and quality people. If Purchasing believes it has a complete right to buy from whomever it wishes, if Engineering feels its responsibilities end in the development laboratory and that the preparation of purchasing specifications is a dull chore to be avoided and Quality thinks its job is to reject parts and materials at incoming inspection, there can be no basis for a supplier quality-control programme. Half of the problems associated with purchased parts and materials are the fault of the customer, not the supplier and these can only be solved by co-operation of the relevant departments.

SUPPLIER APPROVAL

Quality control of suppliers can be divided into three phases: (*a*) selection and approval of suppliers; (*b*) qualification of particular items from particular suppliers; (*c*) continuing quality assurance as product is delivered. These activities interact and they are all affected by previous experience. Usually, there is a decision to change or improve an existing supplier quality-control system because previous results have been unsatisfactory or the volume of purchasing has grown. Only rarely is there a need to start a supplier quality-control system from scratch.

This section will deal with supplier approval, but the applicability of the techniques discussed is affected by prior knowledge of the supplier. It may be quite unnecessary to include in a newly established supplier-survey programme suppliers who have been delivering conforming goods for several years.

The aim of a supplier-approval programme is to draw up a list of approved suppliers who are known to be capable of delivering products in particular categories. Such a programme will normally start with a review of existing suppliers. In some circumstances, the only practical approach will be to grant all or most of the existing suppliers provisional approval so that purchasing can continue. Some of the suppliers will be given full approval on the basis of their history of previous deliveries and others, and new suppliers, will start to be approved or disapproved on the basis of supplier surveys.

It is very difficult to make an accurate judgement of a supplier on the basis of a survey. Occasionally, the company visited will be obviously inadequate, lacking the essential facilities and people to do the job. More often there is nothing that unequivocally disqualifies the supplier. Large companies that have been in business for many years are particularly unlikely to fail clearly a supplier survey. To be worth while a supplier survey must be made by a mature, high-level quality engineer, with the full co-operation of the purchasing department. An extremely important aspect of a supplier survey is that it gives a means of getting over to the supplier's management the message that conforming products really are required and that the customer is himself prepared to go to much trouble to get them. The supplier will judge the customer, to a considerable extent, by the competence and stature of the surveyor.

A survey can often be done most effectively in the context of a contract to purchase particular items. In this case the methods to be used in qualifying the actual items and the methods of continuing quality assurance can be covered simultaneously.

The surveyor will normally complete a printed supplier quality-survey report. This serves as a check list ensuring that all required points are covered. It also makes easier cross-comparison of different suppliers. The report will cover the following factors:

(*a*) management competence;
(*b*) understanding of contract and purchasing specifications;
(*c*) plant and facilities;
(*d*) processes;
(*e*) employee skill;
(*f*) quality-department organization and effectiveness;
(*g*) references.

A direct assessment of management competence and attitude is important. The general manager and his department heads should impress as knowing their business. They should have a clear understanding of the contract and specifications. Moreover, their attitudes to quality should be positive. They should demonstrate a willingness and determination to supply product that conforms exactly to the requirement. If management attitudes are wrong there can be little confidence that conforming products will be supplied. Although the customer can help or hinder the supplier in achieving conforming product the main effect must come from the supplier's own quality system. All of the customer's work on supplier control, source inspection, incoming inspection, feedback of information, etc., will be ineffective with a supplier who does not care about conforming product.

The plant facilities are among the easier factors to assess. The supplier must have the plant needed to manufacture at the required tolerances and level of control. He must also have the necessary test and inspection equipment, including, if required, environmental and reliability test facilities. And, of course, he must have enough of the equipment to satisfy all his commitments.

Where particular processes are involved, such as plating, heat treatment and complex chemical processes used in the manufacture of, for example, electronic components, reproducible, conforming product will only be made if each process is specified in detail and controls are applied to ensure that the specifications are adhered to. Except where proprietary information is involved the surveyor can himself check that processes are performed in conformance to specification.

The skill of the people actually manufacturing the product obviously has a major influence on its quality. Assessment of their skill can best be done by meeting some of them, by talking to them and by examining some of their work.

The effectiveness of the supplier's quality department will also be assessed, both for its own competence and also for its influence on the organization as a whole. The supplier's quality manual can be of considerable assistance in making this assessment. The manual will usually start with a statement of the company's quality policy. As noted in Chapter 1, this should express the general manager's intention to supply exactly conforming product. Organization charts of the company and the quality department will normally be included and these can be evaluated in the light of the principles of quality-department organization discussed in Chapter 3. The major part of the manual will consist of the documentation of the various procedures used by the company in controlling the quality of its product. Effective quality control is difficult in the absence of precise and definite methods of working, so that ensuring the company has well-organized, written and approved procedures is an important aspect of the competence of a quality department. Table 7.1 lists some of the procedures that should be included in a quality manual, either directly or by reference to, for example, technical or comptroller's manuals. The list is not exhaustive. On the other hand, some of the procedures listed may be irrelevant to particular suppliers or sub-contractors. Assessment of the manual itself is insufficient. It is, of course, necessary to check that the procedures included are, in fact, being followed.

The importance of the quality manual can be over-emphasized. For a small company with limited quality-control staff, compilation of a quality manual is not of first priority. Work on inspection and test planning, defect reporting and corrective action, for example, should have higher priority. For this reason, complete absence of a quality manual would not necessarily prevent the approval of a supplier of some items.

One other factor can be of great assistance in deciding whether or not a supplier can be approved. This is the availability of references from other customers of the supplier. These should be asked for and followed up with the quality departments of the other customers. A special kind of reference is where the supplier has official approval from some specialized agency, e.g. the quality-assurance organization of a government department.

TABLE 7.1

List of Procedures included in the Quality Manual

1 *Inspection and Test Procedures*
- 1.1 Incoming
- 1.2 Fabrication and machine shop
- 1.3 Assembly
- 1.4 Final
- 1.5 Packaging and shipping
- 1.6 100% and sampling inspection
  Rules for making lots
  Definition of defects
- 1.7 Control of inspection status
  Procedures for inspection and test stamps
  Product traveller tickets

2 *Quality Engineering*
- 2.1 Responsibility for inspection and test planning
- 2.2 Procedures for collecting, analysing and reporting defect information
- 2.3 Product-quality audit procedures
- 2.4 Corrective-action procedures
- 2.5 Material-review board procedures and responsibilities
- 2.6 Maintenance of Quality records

3 *Supplier Quality*
- 3.1 Responsibility and procedures for supplier and sub-contractor surveys
- 3.2 Source-control and source-inspection procedures and responsibilities
- 3.3 Analysis and feedback of data on supplier quality

4 *Procedures of other Departments*
- 4.1 Contract and specification review procedures
- 4.2 Drawing, specifications and change-control procedures
- 4.3 Design-review procedures
- 4.4 Qualification-test procedures and responsibilities
- 4.5 Quality-cost measuring procedures
- 4.6 Inspection and test-equipment calibration procedures and schedules
- 4.7 Operator-training systems and certification
- 4.8 Corrective-action procedures
- 4.9 Process-specification references for
  welding
  soldering
  plating
  heat treatment
  forgings, etc.
- 4.10 Storage, packaging and transportation responsibilities and procedures

QUALIFICATION APPROVAL

A supplier may have been shown to be generally satisfactory either by survey or by having a record of delivering conforming product. However, it may be necessary to carry out a special exercise on a new product or one that the supplier has not delivered before to confirm that the supplier can achieve conformance to the requirements of that product. When this has been proved, the product from the supplier will be given "qualification approval".

Organizationally, the simplest method of deciding whether or not a part can be given qualification approval is for the customer to obtain samples of the product and test them in his own laboratory. This method is commonly used when, for example, component qualification is the sole responsibility of the technical department without participation from the quality department. Another method is to require the supplier to carry out a specified series of tests and inspections to check conformance to the specification and to report in detail the results obtained. A third method is to rely on the results of tests carried out as part of a national or international quality-control system. This last method will be discussed further later in this chapter in the context of systems used for electronic components. Each of the first two methods has advantages and disadvantages. The main advantages of the customer doing his own testing are that there is no necessity to get the agreement of the supplier and that there is no difficulty in ensuring the honest performance of the tests and reporting of the results. The functional performance of the part can be checked when assembled into the product and also an "open-ended" investigation of the part can be made. The method does not itself demand careful specification of the required performance of the part and the tests to be performed. The specification discipline must therefore be exercised independently and the test results must be related to the specifications. If this is not done, qualification approval can be granted on the basis of good functional performance from the samples, because these happened to have necessary but unspecified characteristics. As the latter are unspecified there is, of course, no assurance that later samples will perform as well. Another disadvantage of the customer doing his own qualification testing is that it necessitates his establishing and staffing a qualification-test laboratory. The cost of this for competent staff and test equipment to cover adequately a full range of parts can be very high. These disadvantages are overcome where the supplier is required to carry out the qualification tests. Obviously he can only be expected to perform specified tests which correspond to specified requirements of the part. This method therefore demands careful evaluation of the function of the part by the user's engineers to determine what are its required characteristics and then careful specification. The supplier will usually already have, for his own control needs, the required test equipment and competent staff. The main problem with this method (apart from the fact that some suppliers will not agree to do the tests or ask an unreasonable price) is that of ensuring that the samples tested are representative of normal production (and have not been specially made or screened) and that the tests are performed and reported honestly. A representative of the customer's quality department will normally witness the tests as a means of validating the results.

CONTINUING QUALITY ASSURANCE

The last stage of quality control of suppliers concerns the continuing assurance of conformance of a series of deliveries of parts or materials. There are three ways of doing this: incoming inspection, source inspection and source control. For incoming inspection the parts are inspected, usually by sampling according to a specified AQL (see chapter 6), when received at the customer's factory. Lots of parts that pass the inspection go into store for use in the factory. Failed lots, which do not conform to specification, should be returned to the supplier for correction. More often than not, especially in modern industry with its emphasis upon close control of inventory, this puts the user into considerable difficulty. The parts are needed and if they are returned to the supplier work may have to be stopped on a product line and also delivery schedules may be jeopardized. Two other alternative courses of action can be taken: (*a*) use the parts as they are; (*b*) for the user himself to sort or re-work the non-conforming parts. The "use-as-is" decision may be correct if the only effect of the non-conformance of the part is to add to the user's cost, but not affect the conformance to specification of the end product. If the user can sort or re-work the parts this also obviously increases his costs, but may not affect the quality of the end product. A major disadvantage of these two courses of action is that they put little pressure on the supplier to improve. The supplier should be charged the excess cost caused by his non-conformant product, but often this is not practicable. Whenever possible the non-conformant parts should be returned to the supplier: this is the most effective way of emphasizing the importance the user places on receiving conformant parts.

The results of the incoming inspection should be tabulated and analysed by part number and by supplier. The quality department should supply this information to the purchasing department in a form that helps the latter to take action, e.g. by giving each week or month the record of the worst five or ten suppliers. The actions to be taken should be agreed at regular meetings between Purchasing and Quality.

An alternative to incoming inspection is source inspection. In this method the user has one or more resident inspectors at the supplier's plant. Each lot of parts is inspected and tested by these resident inspectors and they have responsibility for accepting or rejecting each one. This method is used by major purchasers of parts and complete equipments and systems, who are often government agencies. Such an agency may employ in total many hundreds of staff engaged mainly on source inspection. The advantages of this method are that the time period for rejection, re-work and re-submission are much reduced compared with incoming inspection, and the source-inspection group become expert in the producer's work and may serve a number of different users, who do not therefore need to build up this expertise individually. Another advantage is that use can be made of the supplier's specialized inspection and test equipment. One disadvantage of the method is its cost—incoming inspection is also expensive but, for a given amount of inspection, source inspection will almost certainly cost more. A second disadvantage is that it tends to reduce the supplier's total responsibility for supplying conforming product. No final inspection and test system will ever give complete control of product quality. In actuality the people designing and manufacturing the product must have the major effect, and source inspection suggests a reduction in their responsibility. The user can magnify this problem by attacking his own source inspectors when use of the parts shows them to be defective, rather than concentrating his efforts on the supplier.

Because of the disadvantages of source inspection many of the major purchasers of equipment such as the British Post Office and the Ministry of Defence are relying less on source inspection and more on source control. In the latter system the supplier is made entirely responsible for supplying product conforming to the specifications and in addition he is also made responsible for measuring the conformance level of the product and analysing and reporting these data to the user in a way that gives the latter assurance of the conformance. The efforts of the user's quality staff—their titles are changed from inspectors to emphasize the change of function—are then directed at ensuring that the supplier has the necessary organization, skills and facilities to produce conforming product. Direct inspection or test of the product is carried out only for the purpose of checking the correctness of the methods used by the supplier's quality department. Responsibility for the acceptance and rejection of the product is given explicitly to the supplier's quality department. The advantages of source control over source inspection or incoming inspection are obvious. However, it does demand a higher level of responsibility from the management of the suppliers and a realization that their own long-term advantage is not served by forcing out product that does not really conform to the requirement—however painful the short-term consequences of rejection.

ELECTRONIC PARTS OF ASSESSED QUALITY

This chapter will be concluded with a brief account of a system that is now coming into operation for the quality control of electronic components. It is of interest because it represents probably the most ambitious system of quality control of suppliers ever attempted and at the same time exemplifies many of the features of modern supplier quality control. There have, of course, been quality-control systems applied to the purchase of electronic components for many years, the most widely applied being based upon the Military Standards of the USA. In Europe there have been similar systems based, for example, on DEF specifications and CV specifications in the UK and the CCTU specifications in France. These systems have been applied in the main to the purchase of components for incorporation in military equipment for national Governments. To a lesser degree similar systems have been applied in the civil field, e.g. by the British Post Office for components for its telecommunications equipment.

A committee was set up by the British Government under the chairmanship of Rear-Admiral Burghard and including representatives of the trade associations of the makers of electronic components and non-Government users, together with representatives of Government users. The committee's report recommended that an overall system for the standardization of the specifications for electronic parts should be established. At the same time a comprehensive system for the quality assurance of such parts should be set up. The joint system should be such that it was applicable to most of the electronic components bought by the UK Government for both civil and military use and also to professional industrial requirements. It should *not* be applicable only to sections of the electronics industry making military and similar equipment. It was also recommended that the organization of the system should be vested in the British Standards Institution, an agency representing both makers and users of electronic components and the British Government.

By 1973 the system has developed in three different areas. First, a complete and integrated series of specifications for electronic components is being published—the BS 9000 series. Second, a very advanced system of quality assurance has been set up to ensure that components sold as conforming to particular specifications in the BS 9000 series do in fact conform. Third, an organization has been established under the BSI to control the system.

The specifications are of five main types:

(*a*) A small number of general specifications such as BS 9000 itself, which deal with the system as a whole and are applicable to all components.

(*b*) What are called "generic" specifications. These are general specifications which apply to a particular family of components, e.g. transistors. The generic specifications include methods of test and inspection applicable to the family of components and also rules which define exactly how the "detail" specifications must be written and what they must contain.

(*c*) Two types of detail specifications. These define what the component must do and also emphasize an exact definition of the tests and inspections the component must pass as a means of giving assurance that it does in fact perform according to specification. The two types of detail specifications differ only in the body originating them. Some of the detail specifications are originated by technical committees of the British Standards Institution as a means of achieving standardization. Others are originated by particular component makers themselves (following the rules of the generic specifications). The BS 9000 detail specifications are not much concerned with defining how the components must be made or indeed with what they shall be (except with regard to some external dimensions, lead positions, etc., which affect the use). These are left to the definition of each component maker. BS 9000 specifications are largely concerned with what the component must do and how this shall be tested (see Chapter 1).

(*d*) The fifth type of specification is called a "certified test record". This defines a method by which test and inspection results must be analysed and reported to customers every six months.

An extract from a typical BS 9000 detail specification is given in Table 7.2. This extract defines the tests and inspections that must be carried out. The emphasis is entirely upon sampling inspection (see Chapter 6) and for each sub-group of tests the inspection level and AQL are defined, for application according to BS 9001. Tests in Groups A and B must be performed on every lot and the lot cannot be released until these tests have been passed. Groups A and B therefore define a lot-acceptance procedure. The tests in Groups C and D are not carried out on every lot, but only at longer intervals—every 13 weeks for Group C tests and possibly only every two years or some other long period for Group D tests. Groups C and D therefore define

TABLE 7.2

Inspection Requirements from a Typical Detail Specification used in the System for Electronic Parts of Assessed Quality based on BS 9000. The Actual Specification refers to a General Purpose Signal Diode.

INSPECTION REQUIREMENTS

All tests shall be made at 25 ± 2°C unless otherwise stated (see 1.2.4.1.5. of BS 9300: 1969)

Inspection	BS 9300: 1969 reference and conditions of test		Symbol	Limits		Units
				min.	max.	
GROUP A		Subgroups A3, A4 and A5 not applicable				
Subgroup A1 Visual inspection	1.2.2	*Inspection level I, AQL 1·5%*				
Subgroup A2 Forward voltage Reverse current	 1001 1002	*Inspection level II, AQL 0·65%* I_F = 100 mA V_R = 150 V	 V_{F1} I_{R1}	 — —	 1·2 0·1	 V μA
GROUP B		Subgroups B4, B5 and B6 not applicable				
Subgroup B1 Dimensions	1.2.3	*Inspection level S–2, AQL 6·5%* Ref. BS 3934.SO–6	ϕD G	— —	2·71 7·62	mm mm
Subgroup B2(a) Solderability	1.2.6.10	*Inspection level S–4, AQL 4·0%* See Note 1				
Subgroup B2(b) Rapid change of temperature followed by Damp heat, cyclic	1.2.6.7 1.2.6.3	*Inspection level S–4, AQL 4·0%* T_{amb} −55°C to 100°C Six cycles				
Subgroup B3 Lead fatigue	1.2.6.11.1	*Inspection level S–3, AQL 6·5%* Destructive test See Note 2				
Subgroup B7 Electrical endurance	1.2.7.2	*Inspection level S–4, AQL 1·5%* V_R = 150 V Duration = 160 h min. T_{amb} = 100°C				
Post-test end-points for subgroups B2(b) and B7 Forward voltage Reverse current	 1001 1002	 I_F = 100 mA V_R = 150 V	 V_{F1} I_{R1}	 — —	 1·3 0·2	 *V* μA
Subgroup B8 CTR information	1.1.11	Attributes information for subgroup B2(*a*), B2(*b*), B3 and B7				
GROUP C		Subgroups C2(*a*) and C4 not applicable				
Subgroup C1 Dimensions	1.2.3.	*Inspection level S–2, AQL 6·5%* Ref. BS 3934, SO–6	ϕB_2 L H	0·458 26·0 56·7	0·558 — —	mm mm mm

NOTE 1. When method 1.2.6.10.2 is used, the inspection level shall be reduced to S–3.
NOTE 2. Samples subjected to destructive tests shall not be accepted for release (see 2.6.5 of BS 9000 1967).

INSPECTION REQUIREMENTS (*continued*)

Inspection	BS 9300: 1969 reference and conditions of test		Symbol	Limits		Units
				min.	max.	
Subgroup C2(b)		*Inspection level I, AQL 2·5%*				
Forward voltage	1001	I_F = 15 mA	V_{F2}	0·65	—	V
Forward voltage	1001	I_F = 0·1 mA	V_{F3}	—	0·75	V
Reverse current	1002	V_R = 150 V T_{amb} = 100°C	I_{R3}	—	5	μA
Subgroup C3		*Inspection level S–2, AQL 6·5%*				
Vibration swept frequency followed by	1.2.6.5	f = 150–2000 Hz Acceleration = 196 m/s^2				
Acceleration, steady state	1.2.6.6	Acceleration = 196 km/s^2, direction Y1, Y2 Case mounted, cathode inwards				
Subgroup C5		*Inspection level S–3, AQL 4·0%*				
Electrical endurance	1.2.7.2	V_R = 120 V Duration = 2000 h min. T_{amb} = 100°C				
Post-test end-points for subgroups C3 and C5						
Forward voltage	1001	I_F = 100 mA	V_{F1}	—	1·3	V
Reverse current	1002	V_R = 150 V	I_{R1}	—	0·2	μA
Subgroup C6						
CTR information	1.1.11	Attributes information for subgroup C3 Measurements information for I_{R1} before and after the test in subgroup C5				
GROUP D		Subgroup D2 and D3 not applicable				
Subgroup D1		*Inspection level S–2, AQL 6·5%* See Note 3				
Dimensions	1.2.3	Ref. BS 3934, SO–6	L_1	—	2·54	mm
Subgroup D4		*Inspection level S–3, AQL 4·0%* See Note 3				
Electrical endurance	1.2.7.2	V_R = 120 V Duration 8000 h min. T_{amb} = 100°C				
Post-test end-points for subgroup D4						
Forward voltage	1001	I_F = 100 mA	V_{F1}	—	1·3	V
Reverse current	1002	V_R = 150 V	I_{R1}	—	0·2	μA
Subgroup D5						
CTR information	1.1.11	Measurement information for I_{R1} before and after the test in subgroup D4				

NOTE 3. AQL values are for qualification approval purposes only (see 1.1.10 of BS 9300: 1969).

a quality-audit system: they do not control lot acceptance directly but various actions must be initiated by the management of the component maker in the event of failure. The tests in Groups A, B, C and D include tests of functional performance, visual characteristics, environmental tests and life tests.

The methods of quality assurance which are part of the overall system involve all three phases of supplier quality assurance: supplier approval, component qualification, continuing quality assurance. The emphasis throughout is on supplier control, and incoming inspection and source inspection are not used. The British Standards Institution has appointed the Electrical Quality Assurance Directorate of the Ministry of Defence to be its agent and perform the duties of a supervising inspectorate. Component makers wishing to sell electronic components of a particular family covered by a generic specification, after applying to the British Standards Institution, are subjected to a supplier-survey procedure by a member of the supervising inspectorate. This survey utilizes the methods discussed earlier in this chapter, including evaluation of the contents and application of the supplier's quality manual. Particular emphasis is placed upon the organizational position, professional competence and integrity of the supplier's chief inspector because he is personally responsible for ensuring that the requirements of the system are complied with precisely.

A component maker who is approved for a particular family of parts can then go on to the next phase, which is to get qualification approval for a part conforming to a particular detail specification. To do this he must make and test three lots of the part. In principle, each lot must pass the Group A and B tests of the detail specification and the first lot must pass the Group C and D tests (but special conditions apply to tests taking a long time for completion). The tests are *not* carried out by the supervising inspectorate or any other outside agency. They are carried out by the component maker under the control of his chief inspector, although the latter may sub-contract some of the tests to a "test house" approved under the scheme. Qualification approval is dependent only upon achieving conformance to the Group A, B, C and D tests of the specification.

The continuing quality assurance uses the source-control method exclusively. For each lot, the supplier must extract the samples required by the detail specification and test them in the specified way. If the tests are passed the lot is released. The supervising inspector will visit the plant on a regular basis and sometimes witness tests. He may himself carry out a small number of tests for the purpose of checking methods but will not directly release product. A released lot will normally go into a "bonded" store under the control of the chief inspector and may then be sold to any customer as conforming to the appropriate BS 9000 specification. A principal aim of the system is to remove from each of these customers the necessity for carrying out his own incoming inspection—or indeed the individual application of any of the supplier quality-control procedures.

BSI has set up the necessary organization to run this system and an important part of this organization is a series of standing committees representing Government and non-Government users and the component makers. One of these committees is particularly concerned with the specifications and another with the quality-assurance system including the control of the supervising inspectorate.

The system described above is being devised and applied in the UK. However, during the past few years the necessary steps have been taken to enable a similar system to be used jointly in many European countries. The organizing body for this is CENEL (the European Co-ordinating Committee for Electrical Standards). More recently the decision has been taken to set up a completely international system, organized by the International Electrotechnical Commission (IEC).

8 Quality Control of New Products

Quality control of new products is probably the most difficult and yet the most important branch of the whole subject. Customers in general have a great suspicion of entirely new products. They are attracted by the improved performance, advanced styling and protection against obsolescence of the new model. And the glamour of newness and the interest of technical innovation have an important appeal, making the previous model seem dull and old-fashioned. However, customers also know that "you always have trouble with a new product", and the more self-controlled customers will not buy immediately but will "give them a year or two to get the bugs out".

If new products are a trouble to the customer they may be a disaster to the supplier. The individual customer rejecting a defective product because it does not achieve the advertised performance or returning it because of early reliability failures (see Chapter 9) is seriously inconvenienced. The supplier may have to call in and retrofit thousands of items of the product, and he may not know how to achieve the required improvement. Even if he does the method may be expensive so that costs are increased and profits turned into losses. At the same time he is trying to continue to manufacture the product and simultaneously introduce the required design changes, without throwing his production control and purchasing into chaos.

The successful introduction of new products has always been difficult, but modern competitive pressures intensify the difficulty for two reasons. First is the continuing reduction in the time allowed. The marketing people will not accept a slow development ("the product will be obsolescent before it is launched") and this prevents a meticulous and painstaking development. Secondly, there is the emphasis on cost control. The market will support only a certain price so the product cost is strictly limited. This inhibits the over-design and use of safety margins, which were the saviour of new products in the past.

It is usually impossible to *know* how much money it will cost and how much time it will take to complete the creative development of a new product. So, manufacturing and sales plans are based on estimates. The estimates are usually optimistic: the marketing people are convinced that if the new product is ready by a particular date they can guarantee good sales, but a few months later and all will have gone to a competitor. The development people are worried by the problems they can see, but solutions are already half formed in their minds and as a breed they are optimistic. (It is the problems that they had not anticipated at all that eventually cause the real trouble.) Also if they insisted on a completely realistic or even pessimistic forecast of the time and money to complete the development it is quite possible the project would be seen to be of doubtful profitability and might never be allowed to start. This is the last thing the development people want; they are already fascinated by the technical problems and at the worst they might be out of a job. General management, while discounting to some extent the market forecasts of the sales group and the optimism of the design group, are reluctant to extend the scheduled development time. Extending the time will increase the cost proportionately and will give Marketing a complete alibi for subsequent failure to meet sales forcasts. And they have the feeling that if they extend the allowed development time the pressure and urgency on the design group will be reduced.

For all these reasons, optimistic estimates of development times are all too frequent. As the development goes late the tendency is to cut more and more corners and to gamble progressively that the later stages will take less than the scheduled time. The testing programme is the aspect of the development that is most likely to suffer. The engineers always feel that the product they have developed must work so, when time is short, the testing, which does not really add anything, is the natural thing to cut.

The consequence of all of this was described at the start of the chapter: dissatisfied customers, chaotic manufacturing and lost profits.

There is no way of eliminating this problem other than opting out of development completely and certainly quality control cannot pretend to give an answer. In the main, application of the techniques of quality control will serve only to reveal and clarify the problems earlier than would otherwise happen, so that necessary decisions are made sooner and losses are minimized. Quality control cannot enable a three year development to be completed in two or ensure that a product which has been tested only superficially and informally will conform to all of its requirements. None the less, the contribution of quality control to new-product development is of key importance.

There are three main areas of quality participation in development: (*a*) secondment of quality engineers to the development team, (*b*) design review techniques, (*c*) qualification testing.

Quality Engineers in Development

In Chapter 1 it was stated that the most useful definition of "quality" was conformance to requirements. If this viewpoint is adopted it follows that the development team for a new product is responsible for making it meet all of its requirements both primary and secondary. The team's responsibility does not stop when the product achieves its principal performance requirements and they cannot hand over to some other group, for example of quality engineers, to add the "quality". Similarly, there is little point in including some quality engineers in the development team with the task of "ensuring, right from the beginning, that the quality is built in". It is a basic responsibility of the whole development team to ensure that the new product conforms to all of its requirements, and the presence of quality engineers, as such, in the development team may obscure that responsibility.

Despite the caution expressed above, experienced engineers with a quality background can be useful members of a development team provided they are assigned specific tasks for which they have technical expertise and are not given a general responsibility for "quality". Areas in which quality engineers may be technically expert include: environmental engineering—a knowledge of the environmental stresses, temperature, shock, etc.—which the product must be able to withstand and how this is to be achieved; standards of workmanship that are applicable; components engineering—a knowledge of components, their characteristics and specifications, etc. Another important area, which will be dealt with in the next chapter, is reliability. A satisfactory development may require that such topics are covered exhaustively by technically competent engineers. Whether these engineers are permanent members of the development department or are seconded temporarily from the quality department is not important.

Inspection and test planning must also be a major concern of quality engineering during the development phase. Just as the production engineers will be determining the manufacturing methods to be used and the manufacturing costs, the methods of test and inspection must be defined and specified before the start of manufacturing, and the necessary test and inspection equipment provided. It may also be necessary for staff to be specially trained in new test and inspection methods.

Design Review

Every new product starts out as a basic idea that is progressively elaborated and defined. Before design or development can start, the initial idea must have become at least a written description of the product including its main functions, a tentative estimation of its cost or selling price and the time needed to bring it to the market.

At this stage approval may be given for the development to start, a development team will be assigned to it and money budgeted. In principle, total responsibility for the project could be assigned to the head of the development team with no outside monitoring or control, the expectation being that a complete package of drawings and specifications would be handed over to Manufacturing and Marketing at the scheduled time. In practice, of course, there must be collaboration between the development team and other groups concerned with launching the new product. General management also will want to have methods of monitoring the progress of the development. For both of these general management can leave the initiative entirely with the development group, expecting them to establish the necessary contacts informally with Marketing, Production Engineering, Cost Accounting, Quality Engineering and so on, and relying on the reports issued by the development group itself for assessing progress. While it is not impossible that a particular development project leader will himself obtain the required collaboration from busy and probably critical colleagues in other departments and also report objectively on the progress, or lack of it, of his own team, it is certain that many will not.

Unwilling to accept the self-assessment of the development leader, the responsible general manager may attempt to assess the project by a detailed personal examination of the drawings and models and by questioning the development team. This method has the advantage of making the development team carefully examine its own position as a preparation for the meeting with the manager, but the latter is unlikely to have either the time or technical expertise really to evaluate the project, so any decisions he takes will be to a large extent arbitrary rather than objective.

The design-review system was established to provide a solution to the problems posed above. The general manager requires the head of the development team to schedule and organize a series of formal design reviews. Members of the development team and members of other departments concerned with the project are obligated to participate in these meetings.

The series of design reviews will contain reviews of three types. The initial design review should take place at the concept stage and the people mainly concerned are from Marketing and Engineering. At this meeting the product definition is reviewed, including the primary functions it must perform, secondary functions which are either essential or desirable, and requirements for reliability, maintainability and environmental capability. At the same time the intended market is reviewed including the expected sales volume in different parts of the market. The expected cost and price of the product are reviewed and the schedule for the critical stages in its development and launching.

Intermediate design reviews are scheduled at appropriate time intervals. At these meetings participation is extended to include manufacturing engineering, purchasing, cost accounting and quality engineering. In some units, where manufacturing engineering and quality engineering are not responsible for particular topics such as plant and tooling, test equipment, packaging, components engineering, reliability and training, the relevant departments also must be involved.

The last of the series of design reviews is the final design review at which the completion of the development is assessed and the manufacturing and marketing programme reviewed in the light of the final product specifications, the final costs and the results of qualification testing.

All these reviews are chaired by a senior manager from the technical function, but it is best if the administration of the meetings and their reporting is done by someone independent of the development team. A member of the quality department may be an appropriate choice, because of the emphasis the quality discipline places upon clear and objective reporting. Attendance at the design review should be kept fairly small, say in the range eight to fifteen, and non-participating observers should not be present, as free discussion is inhibited at a big meeting. In large companies, headquarters staff may wish to participate and this has advantages, particularly where the unit members may be inexperienced in design-review procedures, but again the number should be limited.

About two weeks before the meeting the development team should issue a pre-meeting report covering each agenda item, to assist the efficient running of the meeting. Other departments having major contributions to make, either as a result of requests from the development team or because of "actions" accepted at previous reviews, should also issue pre-meeting reports.

After each design review the secretary should send a report to the general manager. This should give a succinct, clear account of the progress of the design against schedule, including the completion of actions previously assigned, and also a list of new actions. The fact that all participants in the review receive copies helps to ensure that the report objectively describes the meeting.

Introduction of an effective design-review system is not easy. Members of the technical department may resent the requirement to present their work for review by colleagues in other departments and also dislike the clarity with which such reviews will reveal slippages in the development schedule. They may also have a superiority complex and feel the other departments have little contribution to make. Members of other departments may have feelings of inferiority in an unaccustomed environment and may become spectators rather than participants, or may over-compensate and criticize the designers rather than constructively assist in the solution of the problems. For these reasons it is necessary for the general manager, once a policy to hold formal design reviews is made, to give sufficient attention to the design-review programme to ensure that the policy is implemented.

From the above description it is clear that the purposes and objectives of design review are concerned with virtually all aspects of the introduction of a new product. The quality aspects of conformance to requirements and minimization of quality costs are only part of this concern. The quality-department participation at the review should be particularly directed at: (*a*) full, complete and formal definition of the requirements of the product, including secondary characteristics, reliability, maintainability, environmental capability, etc.; (*b*) the methods by which conformance to these requirements is to be assured by testing and inspection, including the issue and approval of test and inspection specifications and the procurement of test equipment; (*c*) the overall qualification-test programme (see below); (*d*) component specification and quality assurance; and (*e*) proving of new manufacturing processes and approval of newly trained operators.

Qualification Testing

All new products are subjected to various stages of test and inspection during the development phase. Much testing is carried out informally by the development engineers to show how nearly a required characteristic has been achieved and to point the direction for further development. Testing and inspection also take place routinely during the manufacturing phase, sometimes as part of a final adjustment of the product, and almost always as a means of controlling the proportion of defectives in product going to the customer (see Chapter 2). The manufacturing test and inspection is done against formal test and inspection specifications and procedures, which will be devised during the development phase.

It is possible for the informal testing of the development phase to merge into the routine testing of the manufacturing phase with no particular test event separating the two. Engineering, on the basis of its own information, decides the development is complete and "releases the product" to Manufacturing. The manufacturing-phase testing and inspection is usually inadequate to give high assurance that the product conforms to all of its requirements. It may do no more than ensure that the manufactured product conforms to the engineering design given in the parts list, drawings and process specifications. Functional testing will probably be done to enable adjustments to be made and defects to be identified, but it is unlikely to be exhaustive. Once the manufacture of the product is fully under way, any serious inabilities of the product to meet its requirements will be difficult and expensive to correct. Manufacturing-phase testing has the major disadvantage of taking place too late to be a good tool for revealing major design inadequacies. The development testing is also likely to have deficiencies. Because it is informal it is not possible for its adequacy to be appraised as a whole. Because of the time and money pressures on the development engineers and their confidence in the inherent success of their design it is unlikely to be complete.

Qualification testing is a means of covering the joint inadequacies of development and manufacturing testing and inspection. It arose from the supplier–customer relationship. Before buying a series of products from a supplier, sophisticated customers investigate the supplier's competence and, if satisfied, "approve" the supplier. They also examine the particular product in various ways (see Chapter 7) and again, if satisfied, grant the product "qualification approval" and include it on a "qualified products list". A particular type of qualification approval applies where the supplier has contracted to develop and manufacture a new product to meet the customer's specification. The customer may require that the development is not judged complete and manufacturing may not start until he has declared the product "qualified". The customer usually bases his decision to qualify or not on the results of tests to see if the product's requirements have been met, performed by himself or by an independent laboratory or by the supplier. Such tests are called "qualification tests". In this context the qualification tests are defined as an important part of the contract between the supplier and the customer.

In situations where there is no contractual requirement from the customer for qualification tests it is still extremely useful for the development of a new product to conclude with formal "qualification testing" as a means of filling the gap between development and manufacturing testing. However, although the tests done and methods employed may be the same, the final result is somewhat different because the concept of declaring a product qualified essentially involves two parties: the supplier and the customer or his agent. For a manufacturer to declare his own product qualified, or to decide that it is not, is an artificial concept. The qualification tests have the purpose of helping the manufacturer to decide whether manufacturing and sales can be started or whether the programme must be delayed while further development takes place.

In essence, qualification testing is a particularly thorough phase of testing carried out on the product when development is complete, to give assurance that the product is satisfactory. One approach is to have an "open-ended" investigation of the product. This is only possible when a group of experts are available, who are independent of the development team, e.g. from an external laboratory. This approach, although it has some advantages, is not generally applicable and will not be discussed further here. Another method is to concentrate on conformance to requirements.

The purpose of qualification testing is then to give assurance by the formal performance of a series of specified tests that the product conforms to every one of its defined requirements.

For qualification testing two kinds of specifications are needed. The first defines exactly what the product must be able to do, what environment it must be able to withstand, what reliability and durability it must have, what external dimensions it must have, and so on. This type of specification should be issued before the start of development and may be revised, and made more precise from time to time during development. It is the primary document that defines to Marketing the product that is being developed for sale. This specification should be mature before the scheduled start of qualification testing, but it can be revised even to take account of the results of the qualification testing. Of course, any reduction in specified performance may have an adverse marketing effect.

Each characteristic in the requirement specification should then be reflected in the qualification-test specification. The tests or inspections that give technically and economically the best methods of assuring that the product has each of its required characteristics should be precisely defined. Included must be the exact method of performing each test and the criteria that determine whether or not it is passed or failed. The number of samples to be tested must also be defined. Where the product can be sold in a number of different configurations the exact configurations to be tested must be defined. Usually, it will not be possible to devise a qualification-test programme that gives a high assurance of conformance to every requirement. Sometimes it will be technically impossible—even the best accelerated life tests rarely give a high assurance of say a thirty-year life requirement. Other times the cost of testing or the time needed for the testing will be unacceptable. In these cases an explicit decision not to perform a particular test must be made and the emphasis for quality assurance directed elsewhere, e.g. by including a conservative safety margin in the design. Even without these limitations qualification testing would be no substitute for good and careful design. On the other hand its limitations do not prevent it from being an extremely useful and important tool.

Before submitting samples of product for qualification testing the development team should be confident from their knowledge of the design and the results of development testing that the samples will pass the qualification tests. Qualification testing should not be limited to aspects of the product about which the development team has doubts; on the contrary, significant doubt of the ability of the product to pass the tests probably indicates that the product is not ready for qualification testing. Experience indicates that, however confident the development team is, on new products some of the qualification tests are failed and corrective action is required. Development-team confidence is not therefore a good basis for omitting particular tests. It must be emphasized: the purpose of qualification testing is *not* to find what is wrong with the product; it is to give confirmation that the product is completely right.

The timing of qualification testing within the development, manufacturing cycle is a matter on which judgement must be exercised. Ideally the samples tested should be made by the final manufacturing methods after the development is complete, and large-scale manufacturing and selling should wait until the tests have been passed. Usually this is not practical. The overall programme cannot be delayed in this way and the investment in manufacturing tools and equipment once made cannot be kept idle. Insistence on exact manufacturing samples for qualification tests also delays seriously the start of corrective action required as a result of failed tests. However, the samples tested should approach as nearly as possible to the product of normal manufacturing. Each deviation will reduce the validity of passed tests and complicate the assessment of the significance of failed tests. Where the samples differ markedly from those expected from normal production, tests should be called development tests, not qualification tests. One answer to this problem is to perform the qualification tests twice, first on pre-production samples and secondly after the start of production, but when the output rate is still low. This, of course, adds to the cost of the qualification testing.

Qualification testing is concerned mainly with the design of the product, but all failures occurring during the testing are of importance. Some will be due to deficiencies of the design. Others may be because the samples tested were not made in accordance with the design. But these latter may indicate particular difficulties in manufacturing a product that does conform to the design. In order to know how well the samples tested conform to the design the qualification testing will normally include a formal check of the samples against the design drawings. The conformance of the samples to applicable workmanship standards will also be inspected. These particular checks have a very important secondary function: they also enable the status of the drawings and standards themselves to be appraised at a defined instant in the development programme. In practice, an extremely important by-product of formal qualification testing is the discipline it applies to the whole development process. Often it is only the demands of the qualification-test programme that ensure complete definition of the product's requirements and the completion of other important specifications and standards. Without qualification testing these problems may be resolved only after major trouble and confusion with customers.

Some of the types of tests that are often included in a qualification-test specification are given in Table 8.1. All products have to operate

TABLE 8.1

Tests Included in a Qualification Test Specification

1	Check of configuration control
2	Check of conformance of samples to design
3	Visual and mechanical inspection of dimensions and workmanship
4	Complete functional testing under normal operating conditions
5	Functional testing under specified marginal-supply conditions
6	Tests of ability to function correctly in specified extreme environments
7	Tests of ability to withstand without damage specified transport and storage environments
8	Reliability tests for life and failure rate
9	Tests of maintainability

satisfactorily within an applicable range of external environments and most products have to be able to withstand without damage particular kinds of transport and storage. Tests for these characteristics are given as items 6 and 7 of Table 8.1. Environmental testing has been the subject of much national and international standardization. Table 8.2 lists the tests that have been standardized by the International Electrotechnical Commission (IEC) in its standard IEC 68, for use on electrical equipment and components. It gives an

TABLE 8.2

List of Tests Included in IEC 68 "Basic Environmental Testing Procedures for Electronic Components and Electronic Equipment"

Test	
A	Cold
B	Dry heat
C	Damp heat (steady state)
D	Damp heat (cyclic)
E	Impact (e.g. shock and bump)
F	Vibration
G	Acceleration (steady state)
H	Storage
J	Mould growth
K	Corrosive atmospheres (e.g. salt mist)
L	Dust and sand
M	Air pressure (high or low)
N	Change of temperature
P	Flammability
Q	Sealing (including panel sealing, container sealing and protection against ingress and leakage of fluid)
R	Unallotted
S	Radiation (e.g. solar or nuclear)
T	Soldering (including thermal shock from soldering)
U	Robustness of terminations
V	Acoustic noise
W,X,Y	Unallotted
Z	Combined tests

indication of the range of environmental tests that may form part of a qualification-test programme. Every event occurring during the qualification testing must be formally reported in a properly controlled test log.

Where qualification tests are carried out as a contractual requirement of the customer it will be usual for the test data to be appraised by the cutomer's quality personnel. The latter will often wish to examine and analyse the primary data and will be prepared to spend a considerable time determining whether or not the product has passed each of the specified tests. In these circumstances the qualification-test report may be very long and detailed. When qualification testing is done by a manufacturer on his own product the requirements of the qualification-test report are different. The results given in the report are a major factor in enabling management to decide that a new product is ready for manufacture and sale. It is therefore very important that the results are reported to management clearly and objectively. The layout and presentation of the report must be such that the important results are highlighted and with enough detail to carry conviction. Also information should be included that will give management assurance of the objectivity of the report. However, the report must be as concise as possible: general managers cannot be expected to work with a large volume of data. Nor should understanding of the report be dependent upon knowledge of various referenced documents, which management will not be familiar with. It must be self-explanatory. Table 8.3 gives an example of the section

TABLE 8.3

Example of Section Headings of a Qualification Test Report

1	Approval signatures
2	Distribution
3	Summary
4	Contents
5	Qualification test personnel
6	Test venue and date
7	Specifications
8	Test samples and configuration tested
9	Test log
10	Summary of test results and status
11	Corrective actions
12	Repeat of failed tests

headings of such a report. Inclusion of the approval signatures, the names of the people who carried out the testing and those responsible for corrective action, the place where the tests were carried out and the dates of the start and end of the test, gives the readers confidence that the report can be believed. Also the fact that they are personally named to their senior management as responsible for the tests emphasizes the importance of the qualification-test exercise to the test personnel.

The summary, in half a page or less, should list the tests passed or failed, the main conclusions of the test and the status of important corrective actions. Under specifications should be given the number, issue number, date and approval status of the requirement specification and qualification-test specification. If possible, a one- or two-page summary of the specifications forms a useful appendix to the report.

The section on test samples and configuration tested should describe precisely the samples tested, their configuration, where and when they were made, whether they were made completely on manufacturing tools, if they were taken from production lots how the sampling was done, etc. The test-log section simply gives the whereabouts of the log, and names the person responsible for its safe keeping. A typical page from the log can also be given as an appendix to the report.

The summary of the test results and status is the heart of the qualification-test report. It is best given in tabular form. For each test in turn it should state whether or not the test has been completed and if so whether it was passed. If it was failed this should be stated and a very brief description given of the reason for failure. The aim should be to give in two or three pages a description of the results which gives the reader a clear view of the overall status of the qualification test.

An account of the further development or re-design performed as a consequence of failure to pass some of the tests is not logically part of the qualification-test report and the people responsible for the tests should be different from the people responsible for the corrective action. However, the readers of the report will get an incorrectly pessimistic view of the situation if they are told of failed tests and are given no account of the progress of work to correct these failures. It is best therefore to include a short summary of the major corrective actions.

All failed tests should be repeated after the defects revealed have been corrected and, in principle, it would be best to repeat all tests, because the changes done to enable one test to be passed may have reduced the ability to pass another test. In practice judgement is usually exercised about the need to repeat all tests. An interim qualification-test report should make it clear which tests are to be repeated and when.

As noted above the concept of qualification testing arose from the customer–supplier relationship and in this context qualification testing applies directly to products that are to be offered for sale. However, even in this context the customer may require, not only that the end item is subjected to qualification testing, but that components and sub-assemblies are individually approved as a result of qualification tests performed on them separately. The customer recognizes that the qualification tests on the end item do not give perfect assurance that it meets all its requirements, and for some of the requirements, e.g. reliability, the level of assurance may be low. The customer therefore shifts part of his quality-assurance activity from specifying what the product should do (requirement specification) and how this shall be tested (qualification testing) to specifying how the product shall be made (it shall be made using qualified parts).

The relationship of these different types of specification was discussed in Chapter 1.

Any complex product can be thought of as a pyramid made in a number of "levels" with basic materials at the bottom level, components at the next level, sub-assemblies at the next and the final end item at the apex of the pyramid. In principle every part at every level could be qualification tested, but this would give great redundancy and, in practice, judgement must be exercised about which parts and levels should be tested in this way. In any case major emphasis should be given to the qualification testing of the end item—this is, after all, what is to be sold to the customer and what contractually must meet specified requirements. The only reasons for qualification testing the parts at lower levels are that it may not be possible to test the end item satisfactorily, e.g. for reliability, and that testing at the lower levels may reveal problems earlier.

The need for emphasis on the testing of the end item is not always appreciated by members of the development team. Psychologically they prefer testing at the lower levels. They are worried that the components they are buying may not perform according to specification and would like to have this checked. They are less keen to have their own work checked and in any case they have great confidence that the latter is satisfactory. An analogous situation occurs when manufacturing personnel are keen for Quality to increase its activity in incoming inspection but less enthusiastic about increased final inspection.

Organization for Qualification Testing

Where a manufacturer is qualification testing his own product, the simplest way to organize this is to establish a separate department solely for this purpose. The department is independent of Design/Development, Manufacturing or Marketing and reports directly to general management. It is provided with the necessary staff and test equipment to carry out the required testing. Samples of all new products are submitted to the department and are only released for manufacturing and sales after successfully passing the qualification tests. This is probably the most effective way of organizing qualification testing. The objections are that it must cost a large amount of money and take a long period of time to establish and build up the qualification-test department. The method is also most applicable when the product range is limited and qualification testing is concerned mainly with successive models each of which will have high sales value, for example computers. Where the product range is very diversified it is difficult to build up expertise for every product.

A variation of this method is to make qualification testing the responsibility of the quality department. This is likely to be less successful, mainly because it does not force management into a recognition of the overall cost of qualification testing as clearly as does the establishment of a separate department. Consequently the resources provided may be inadequate.

Another alternative is to make qualification testing the responsibility of the technical department. This is obviously economical. Much of the required test equipment will be available because of the needs of development testing, and, of course, the deep technical knowledge of the product and its requirements will be present. There are however important objections to this approach. It puts the technical department in the position of judging its own work. However concientiously the engineers try, it will be extremely difficult for them to carry out the tests precisely and report the results objectively. They are mentally too near the product and too emotionally involved with it. Also the important discipline exercised upon the development process by independent qualification testing is lost and the qualification testing may be sacrificed if the development programme goes late.

One way of overcoming some of the objections to having the technical department carry out qualification testing is to make it jointly responsible with the quality department. Usually, divided responsibility leads to confusion and inefficiency and it is therefore important to define precisely the different parts of the overall qualification-testing process for which the two departments are responsible. In broad terms the technical department is responsible for paying for the qualification testing as part of the development budget and providing necessary technical expertise. The quality department is responsible for auditing that all tests are carried out precisely in conformance to defined specifications, that all events occurring during the testing are logged, that no illegitimate interference with the test samples occurs and for preparing interim and final qualification-test reports for presentation to general management. The responsibilities of the two departments are listed in more detail in Table 8.4. It is useful for the technical department and the quality department each to appoint a programme manager for every product to be qualification tested, and many of the responsibilities listed in Table 8.4 will be carried by the two programme managers. Some, however, will be the responsibility of the respective department heads.

The major decisions which must be taken as a consequence of failure of qualification tests should be taken by general management and should not be left to any individual department. Some failures may be trivial and will not warrant any delay to the manufacturing and sales programme, but only rapid and energetic action to correct

TABLE 8.4

Responsibilities of the Technical and Quality Departments for Qualification Testing

Technical Department

1 Decides which new products require qualification testing.
2 Appoints technical programme manager for each product for qualification testing.
3 Includes the cost of qualification testing (and re-testing necessitated by initial failures) as an identifiable item in the development budget. Pays all costs of the tests including the supply of units for test.
4 Includes the necessary time for qualification testing in the development programme.
5 Includes qualification testing as development "milestones" (minimum requirement: start of testing and publication of final qualification-test report).
6 Defines the product configuration to be tested.
7 Defines how the samples for test are to be made and ensures that methods are as near as possible to those of manufacturing.
8 Ensures that the required numbers of samples for test are made and delivered according to schedule.
9 Ensures that staff to carry out tests requiring expertise possessed by the technical department (e.g. functional tests) is available at the scheduled time.
10 Ensures that functional test equipment is available according to schedule.
11 Ensures that the specifications defining the requirements that the product must meet have been written, approved by Technical and Marketing and formally published according to schedule.
12 Ensures that the specifications defining the qualification tests which must be carried out to check each requirement and the results that must be obtained, have been written, approved by Technical and Quality and formally published, according to schedule.
13 Approves the qualification-test schedule.
14 Approves (or formally objects to) qualification-test reports.
15 Corrects the product design to overcome deficiencies revealed by failure of qualification tests.

Quality Department

1 Audits list of products requiring qualification testing and reports to general management unresolved omissions.
2 Appoints quality programme manager for each product for qualification test.
3 Supplies staff to carry out tests and inspections (e.g. visual and mechanical inspections, environmental tests) requiring expertise possessed by the quality department.
4 Takes responsibility for ensuring that all aspects of the qualification test are performed correctly according to schedule or that delinquencies are reported to the general manager.
5 Draws up and publishes the qualification-test schedule.
6 Audits correct performance of the technical department responsibilities and reports to the general manager unresolved delinquencies.

TABLE 8.4 (*contd.*)

Quality Department (*contd.*)

7 Provides Technical with assistance in drafting the qualification-test specification.
8 Approves or formally disapproves of the qualification-test specification.
9 By direct auditing ensures that every test is carried out in conformance to the qualification-test specification.
10 Ensures that the qualification-test log is filled in correctly and is retained for reference.
11 Reports to the general manager monthly on the progress of the qualification tests against the schedule.
12 Writes interim and final qualification-test reports and publishes these to the general manager with copies to Marketing, Technical, Quality and Manufacturing.
13 Audits that corrective actions shown necessary by failure of tests is carried out.
14 Audits that re-testing following corrective action is carried out.

them. Others will require more serious action. The qualification-test reports should clearly define the factual results, but the technical, marketing, manufacturing and quality departments will all have opinions to express on the importance of the failures and their consequences.

General management may decide not to delay the sales programme after failure of a qualification test, provided the failure is judged to be trivial. However, a clear policy should be established by general management that no product is to be delivered to customers until the initial, planned, qualification tests have been completed. Until the tests have been carried out, the extent of the risk in delivery to customers is unknown: failures during test give a level of risk which can be estimated. Insistence on no delivery until the planned tests have been completed also gives a powerful incentive to the development department to schedule and budget the tests properly. Another firm policy should be that the planned qualification tests must not be cut down to compensate for delays in the development programme. It is only by insisting that qualification testing is essential, not just desirable, that in most instances it will actually happen.

ERROR CONTROL IN ENGINEERING

No control system can be a substitute for a high level of technical creativity in design and development engineering. However, only part of the development process is concerned with imaginative creativity and the rest is susceptible to control by different systems. In the main the systems that have been most often applied have been concerned with cost control and schedule control during development and, although there have been many conspicuous failures, there is no doubt that the overall effects of application of these control systems have been beneficial.

The methods of quality control are equally applicable to engineering. Quality control is concerned with errors, defects, defectives and failures, and possibly its most basic technique depends upon quantitative measurement of the number or proportion of these, followed by analysis and systematic performance of corrective actions. The technique is clearly applicable to the more routine parts of the design process. For example, it is common practice for the drawing-office supervisor to check drawings. This is an unsophisticated form of inspection with the purpose of screening out defects on the drawings resulting from errors by the draughtsmen. The effort spent is likely to be more effective if the casual checking with the emphasis upon screening is replaced by controlled sampling with the emphasis upon "prevention". The work of each draughtsman should be sampled in a controlled way and the results recorded and analysed. Often it will be found that a few of the draughtsmen are responsible for the majority of the defects and that special training and motivation of these few gives a big benefit. An overall improvement often results simply as a result of individual draughtsmen knowing their performance. The results also allow an estimate to be made of the cost of allowing the drawing errors to pass on—costs borne in design changes, test fault finding, scrap and re-work.

Such techniques are also applicable to the design engineers themselves, for example, where they are required to apply particular design rules. Analysis of the results of testing of prototypes may also indicate how the engineering errors revealed can be prevented in future designs. In other cases, incorrect application of design rules may not be revealed by testing of prototypes because the rules are concerned with the long-term reliability of the product. In such cases direct inspection of the designs for correct application of the rules may be the only way of ensuring the product has the required reliability.

In Chapter 1 it was stated that in rall human activities error is possible and, in the absence of planned eror prevention, almost inevitable. This is certainly true of design engineering and recognition of this fact should be the first stage in a systematic attempt to control and reduce the number of design errors.

9 Quality and Reliability[1]

To some extent the subject of reliability is looked at in two different ways. On the one hand it is considered as an unspecific part of "quality and reliability". For example, when Britain held its Quality and Reliability Year in 1966/67 the intention of the organizers was to reach as large as possible a section of British industry, and to motivate both managers and individual workers to give greater attention to quality and reliability. But there was no particular emphasis on reliability as a technically special subject, clearly differentiated from quality.

The other side of reliability is represented by a group of specialists, working predominantly in the defence and space industries and concerned particularly with electronics and avionics. Because of the size of these industries in the United States, the reliability specialists there have been able to develop the subject into one of considerable sophistication and the United Kingdom and the rest of Europe have relied heavily on this work. Indeed it is very doubtful if the specialized subject of reliability would have developed to anything like its present degree without the pressure of the American defence and space industries.

Reliability is defined for technical purposes as "the ability of an item to perform a required function under stated conditions for a stated period of time".[2] Although variations of the definition have been published the ideas expressed in the above definition are generally accepted with less controversy than the definition of "quality" (see Chapter 1). The definition of reliability is analogous to the definition of quality adopted in Chapter 1, with its emphasis on conformance. (In fact the definition of quality could almost be re-stated as

[1] Part of this chapter uses material first published in *Electronics and Power*, November 1969.

[2] IEC Publication 271.

"the ability of an item to perform its required functions under stated conditions", except that quality includes conformance to what the item should be, as well as to what it should do.) Reliability is differentiated from quality by being restricted to "ability to perform" and, more importantly, by being particularly concerned with time. The ability to perform "for a stated period of time" is central to reliability.

THE RELIABILITY PROBLEM

In practice, it is the difficulty and cost, both in time and money, of reliability testing that have led to the growth of reliability engineering as a separate discipline.

In the quality control of a new product, there are three important phases:

(i) the establishment and specification of the characteristics that the product must have;

(ii) design and manufacture to achieve the required characteristics;

(iii) testing to show that the required characteristics have been achieved.

These three phases do not occur in simple, consecutive order. The design, development and manufacturing process almost always contains many iterations, because testing at various stages shows the required characteristics have not been achieved. There are continual feedback loops of re-design, re-development and re-work, because of the deficiencies revealed by the testing. As pointed out in Chapter 8 the requirement specification may also be changed as a consequence of the results of testing.

Testing during the development, qualification and manufacturing phases is a key activity and, for a complex product, testing costs may be an important part of the total cost. However, except for the larger systems, testing of the immediate characteristics of an individual item can be carried out in hours or days. Even qualification testing which is the most thorough and elaborate stage of testing rarely takes more than a few weeks. For immediate characteristics, therefore, testing is a very effective process for assisting development and manufacturing and giving assurance that the required characteristics of the product have been achieved.

Reliability presents no special problem when the same three phases can be applied. The required reliability characteristics of the product are defined; design, development and manufacture to meet the reliability are carried out using reliability testing as an iterative tool and finally the reliability of the completed product is tested to give assurance that the required characteristics have been achieved. The difficulty is that often the reliability characteristics required cannot be aligned with a practicable testing programme to check achievement of those requirements.

Because time is an essential part of reliability, measures of reliability are concerned with how often an item fails. If it fails often it is unreliable; if it fails infrequently it is reliable. When a product does not conform to its requirements the first time it is tested or used this is not referred to as a reliability failure. Reliability is concerned with failure to conform after some period of conformance.

For a complex product that can be repaired a common measure of reliability is "mean time between failures". The product is operated "under stated conditions" and after some time it fails "to perform a required function". This event is a failure. The product is repaired and operation is restarted. After a further period of time it fails again. The procedure is continued, the time between failures being measured. The average of these time intervals is the mean time between failures (mtbf) usually measured in hours. The longer the mtbf the better the reliability. Obviously, more than one item of the product can be operated under the stated conditions. The mean time between failures can then be calculated from the results on all of the items.

The mtbf of a particular product will depend upon the stated conditions of operation. If these are made more extreme, for example by requiring the product to operate in a higher ambient temperature, or by increasing the proportion of operating time to waiting time, the mtbf can be expected to be shortened. Similarly, changing the requirements will change the mtbf. For a particular car model the mtbf will have one value if every item of equipment, screen washers, interior lights, etc., is required to perform to specification and a longer value if the requirement is simply that the car can be driven along the road. Finally, even with defined conditions and requirements the mtbf may not remain constant. It may improve because the successive repairs progressively eliminate defective components, or it may deteriorate because the product starts to wear out.

Formally, failure and mean time between failures are defined respectively as follows:[1]

"Failure: the termination of the ability of an item to perform its required function."

"Mean time between failures observed—mtbf (for repairable items)—for a stated period in the life of an item, the mean value of the lengths of observed times between consecutive failures under stated

[1] IEC Publication 271.

stress conditions." IEC 271 gives several associated definitions, but they need not concern us.

For simple, non-repairable items made in large quantities, mean time between failures cannot be used as a measure of reliability, and it is customary to use failure rate. For example, the reliability of an electronic component might be measured by life testing 500 of them in a particular circuit for 1,000 hours. If four units failed, the failure rate would be 0·8 per cent in 1,000 hours (to be exact a small correction should be made to take account of the fact that the four failed devices were tested for less than 1,000 hours). Just as with mtbf, the failure rate is affected by the operating conditions and failure criteria and can change with time because defective units are eliminated from the sample, or because of the onset of wear-out. Sometimes it is convenient to assume that the failure rate does not change with time and if there are neither "early" failures nor wear-out failures this may be virtually correct. The failure rate can then be expressed in reciprocal hours, just as mtbf is measured in hours. The failure rate observed in the life test described above is then given as 8×10^{-6} per hour.

Earlier in this chapter it was said that it was the difficulty and cost of reliability testing that had led to the growth of reliability engineering as a separate discipline. To illustrate the point two reliability requirements are given below—one for a telephone exchange and the other for an electronic component—a general-purpose transistor. The first is quoted from an actual British Post Office specification (TE 1882) and the second is hypothetical but fairly realistic.

(i) Circuit and system design shall be such that the estimated failure rate of equipment within the exchange, including line and digital signalling equipment as well as the switching plant, does not indicate more frequent loss of service on average than the following:

4.1: Individual trunk circuits; loss of incoming or outgoing service once in 10 years

4.2: Service to groups of trunk circuits; loss of incoming or outgoing service to more than 15 per cent of the trunk circuits once in 20 years

4.3: Major breakdowns; loss of incoming or outgoing service to more than 50 per cent of the trunk circuitry once in 50 years.

(ii) During a 5-year period the failure rate of transistor type A shall not rise above $1{\cdot}7 \times 10^{-8}$ per hour. The operating conditions are those of circuits a,b,c,d . . . l,m,n of computer type XYZ123, and the failure criteria are those applicable to the transistor in these circuits. Environmental conditions include a maximum case temperature of 70°C.

In addition, during 3,500h of operation in radio altimeter type ABC987, the failure rate shall not rise above $3{\cdot}4 \times 10^{-8}$ per hour. The operating conditions and failure criteria are defined in terms of the various circuits of the altimeter, and the environmental conditions include a maximum case temperature of 95°C, vibration and temperature cycling.

In addition, during 1,000h of operation in a transistor radio . . .[1]

[1] *Electronics and Power*, November 1969.

It is clearly almost impossible to test directly the reliability requirements exemplified above. The first would require the testing of a model exchange for between ten and fifty years. When the model had been shown to have the required reliability, manufacture and installation of identical exchanges for sale to the Post Office could start. In fact, for statistical reasons, to be fairly confident that the exchanges for sale would have the required reliability several model exchanges would have to be tested.

For the second example, the general purpose transistor, 1,300 transistors would have to be tested for five years in circuit a, with only one failure, to show that the first reliability requirement had been met. (The failure rate = 1 failure divided by 1,300 and 43,680 hours). In practice, a larger sample would be needed both for statistical reasons and also to give assurance that at no time during the five years was the failure rate exceeded. Further tests would have to be done in the other computer circuits and more to test the reliability for the other applications.

The reliability requirement of the telephone exchange is obviously practical and the reliability requirement of the transistor is also reasonable as will become apparent later in the chapter. Some products have reliability requirements that are easy to test. For example, incandescent lamps have a life of 1,000 hours continuous operation under fairly controlled conditions. No serious consequence would occur if, say, 1 per cent failed more quickly than this. A few hundred lamps tested for six weeks would show whether or not the requirement had been met. For a lamp engineer, reliability is just another characteristic to be met. He can quickly test if he has succeeded or not and also have rapid feedback of failure information to assist any required reliability improvement. For some household appliances, e.g. an electric toaster, direct reliability testing is more difficult than for a lamp but still practicable. A television set with a required operating lifetime of 5,000 hours or more is probably at the limit of reliability assurance by direct testing.

For products where the reliability requirement can be easily tested there is little need for specialized reliability engineering. Reliability engineering is a response to situations where the reliability cannot be easily and directly tested. It attempts to provide methods of designing, developing and manufacturing products which have their required reliability without being able to measure the resulting reliability directly and without the design benefits of the feedback of this information. Reliability engineering also provides indirect methods of measuring the reliability of products.

The next four sections of this chapter deal with some of the most important techniques of reliability engineering.

MAKING RELIABLE PRODUCTS

There are various methods of making reliable products. The simplest is just to go on making well-established products which have been shown by long periods of use to have the required reliability. Provided the same materials and methods of manufacture are used the product made today can be expected to have the same reliability as that made ten or twenty years ago. An extension of this philosophy is to design new products but to use components and techniques that have a long history of known reliability. For example, virtually every telephone exchange is different from every other and each one can therefore be considered as a new product. Telephone exchanges are still being made using the Strowger methods that were established forty years or more ago and containing essential components such as relays and selector mechanisms designed almost as long ago. It is unlikely that a new exchange made by these methods would have a reliability very different from that of the others.

In an age of innovation it is not possible for new products to be limited to those that can be made by long-established techniques. Innovation is needed to achieve new performance, to give cost reduction and to meet the customer's subjective desires for change and new fashion. Other techniques for achieving reliability must therefore be adopted. One method of giving feedback to the designer of a new product is to "predict" the reliability of his design rather than measure it.

Reliability prediction depends upon synthesizing the reliability of a product from the known reliability of the parts from which it is made. For example, the design of a central processor unit (CPU) of a computer might include 100 printed circuit boards (see Chapter 4). Each of these boards might contain 50 of a particular type of electronic component known as a semiconductor integrated circuit (SCIC), having 14 leads each of which is attached to the copper track of the board with a solder joint.

Usually the failure of any part will cause a failure of the whole, so if the failure rates of the SCICs and the solder joints are known the failure rate of the computer CPU can be predicted. (Of course, a real computer CPU would have many other component types, which should be included in the reliability prediction but the method can be illustrated using only the SCICs and the solder joints.) Assuming the SCICs have a failure rate of 8×10^{-8} per hour and the solder joints of 2×10^{-9} per hour the number of failures of the computer CPU in one hour should be:

> number of SCIC failures in one hour + number of solder joint failures in one hour

i.e.

number of SCICs × SCIC failure rate + number of solder joints × solder joint failure rate

i.e.

$$(100 \times 50 \times 8 \times 10^{-8}) + (100 \times 50 \times 14 \times 2 \times 10^{-9})$$

i.e.

$$(4 \times 10^{-4}) + (1{\cdot}4 \times 10^{-4}) = 5{\cdot}4 \times 10^{-4}$$

The computer CPU is predicted to have $5{\cdot}4 \times 10^{-4}$ failures in an hour, i.e. a failure rate of $5{\cdot}4 \times 10^{-4}$ per hour. Fortunately, this number is much less than 1, the implication being that the CPU is unlikely to fail in 1 hour. The meaning of the numerical value can be better understood if the reciprocal of the failure rate is taken, this being the mean time between failures (mtbf). The reciprocal of $5{\cdot}4 \times 10^{-4}$ per hour is $0{\cdot}185 \times 10^{4}$ hours. The mean time between failures of the computer CPU is therefore predicted to be 1,850 hours, which is about 11 weeks. The prediction is that computer CPUs made according to this particular design will require repairing because of a failure on average every 11 weeks of operation.

For many applications this might be acceptable and the design could then be proceeded with: for others the mtbf would be too short and the design would have to be improved.

Earlier in this chapter two examples of typical reliability requirements were given, one for a telephone exchange and another for a general-purpose transistor. Modern telephone exchanges are starting to be controlled by computers and it is clear that this computer would not be reliable enough for that application. It is also apparent why the transistor failure rates given in the second example of $1{\cdot}7 \times 10^{-7}$ per hour and $3{\cdot}4 \times 10^{-8}$ per hour are likely to be realistic—failure rates as low as this are needed so that complex electronic equipment of acceptable reliability can be made.

The reliability-prediction calculation makes clear one rule for designing reliable equipment: the importance of simplicity. The failure rate of the computer CPU was directly proportional to the number of components. The point can be illustrated by repeating the calculation for a smaller computer CPU containing only half the number of printed boards, but with all else the same. The number of failures of the smaller computer CPU in one hour is:

Number of SCIC failures in 1 hour + number of solder joint failures in 1 hour i.e.

$$(50 \times 50 \times 8 \times 10^{-8}) + (50 \times 50 \times 14 \times 2 \times 10^{-9})$$

i.e.

$$(2 \times 10^{-4}) + (0{\cdot}7 \times 10^{-4}) = 2{\cdot}7 \times 10^{-4}$$

The predicted failure rate is $2{\cdot}7 \times 10^{-4}$ per hour and the reciprocal, the predicted mean time between failures is 3,700 hours. Halving the number of components doubled the average time the computer CPU would be expected to operate without having to be repaired. The more complicated a thing is the more there is to go wrong and the more likely it is to be unreliable. Conversely, complex objects can only work reliably if the parts from which they are made have very low failure rates.

Reliability prediction would seem to give a very cheap and easy method of checking the reliability of a design and giving feedback of information to the designer. If the predicted mtbf is equal to or better than the requirement the design can continue. If the mtbf is too short the design must be changed and the prediction also will indicate the most fruitful areas for improvement. In our simple example the SCICs contributed three times as much to the failure rate as the solder joints. Improvement should therefore be concentrated on the SCISs. In a real case, where scores or even hundreds of different kinds of components are involved, the reliability prediction will often show that the failure rate of the equipment is dominated by a handful of component types. Changes to all the others will give little improvement which can only come as a result of changes to the key components.

Reliability prediction is a very useful method of giving information feedback to an equipment designer, but it has some major difficulties. In practice, the mathematics is more complicated than just making the "component count", filling in the appropriate component failure rates and calculating the equipment failure rate and mean time between failures. However, the important difficulty is not in the mathematics. The difficulty is in knowing the component failure rates. There are three problems with this:

(i) To measure a component failure rate of 10^{-8} per hour it is necessary to accumulate more than 10^{8} "component hours" of test information. For example 10,000 components could be tested for 10,000 hours (rather more than 1 year). If only one failed in that time the observed failure rate would be 1×10^{-8} per hour. For statistical reasons it would be necessary to do an even bigger experiment and for some components failure rates of 10^{-9} per hour or even better are needed, requiring even larger experiments. Actual tests of this kind are extremely expensive and time-consuming. Of course, component failure-rate information can also be obtained from actual field use of equipment but collecting this information presents its own problems.

(ii) As pointed out earlier in this chapter, the failure rate of a particular component changes markedly, depending upon how much it is stressed and how much it is permitted to degrade before it is unable to fulfill its requirement. Consequently, it is necessary to do even more complicated tests in order to measure the failure rate of the components under different conditions. Also, in the reliability prediction every component must be analysed to see how much it is stressed and how much it can change before causing failure, before inserting the appropriate failure rate.

(iii) Components of exactly the same type used in the same way can have failure rates that differ by 100 times or more. A particular component type might have been made by a manufacturer in the USA in 1968. Its failure rate might have been measured in a large experiment financed by the US Government in 1969. The same type of component to the same performance specification and using basically the same technology but with many process differences is being made by a UK manufacturer in 1972 for use in a UK equipment. Can the USA data be used for a reliability prediction on the UK equipment? The answer may be that there is no other data available, but its use can put major inaccuracies into the prediction.

Good component failure-rate data is rarely available for reliability predictions but despite this the synthesis of equipment mtbf's from component failure-rate data is a very useful technique. It can show that the reliability of a design should easily meet its requirements, or that it is wrong by an order of magnitude. It can show that a particular component type must be replaced by another of especially low failure rate or that stress levels must be reduced.

There are many collections of component failure rate data of which perhaps the best known is the American MIL-HDBK-217A.

REDUNDANCY

A reliability prediction may show that a particular reliability requirement cannot be met by simplifying the design to reduce the component count, by close attention to stress levels and tolerances and by obtaining especially reliable components. Another method of improving reliability is to introduce redundancy. In essence, part or whole of their equipment is duplicated (or re-duplicated) so that failure of one section does not prevent the overall function being performed.

Introduction of redundancy can be a very effective, though expensive, means of improving reliability. The detailed methods are specialized and complex. The redundancy can be introduced at all levels, from duplication of individual components or sub-assemblies to repeats of whole equipments. Redundancy can be active or passive, depending upon whether it is operational continuously or is only switched on after a failure in the primary functional path. Reliability prediction itself is complicated greatly when redundancy is present: no longer is it true that each component failure produces an equipment failure.

Apart from its cost, redundancy can introduce another problem. Incorrectly used it can improve reliability to a disappointingly small degree. This is because redundancy inevitably introduces additional complexity and, as noted above, complexity reduces reliability.

ACCELERATED LIFE TESTING

When it is not practicable because of the needed time and cost to measure the reliability of a product in its normal method of operation it is sometimes useful to use accelerated life testing. An accelerated test is defined[1] as, "A test in which the applied stress level is chosen to exceed that stated in the reference condition in order to shorten the time required to observe the stress response of the item, or magnify the response in a given time. To be valid, an accelerated test must not alter the basic modes and/or mechanisms of failure, or their relative prevalence."

By definition, the result of the accelerated test is not of direct interest. What is of interest is a deduction, based on the accelerated test, of the reliability of the product under its normal use condition ("the reference condition"). The simplest kind of accelerated test is done by changing the "duty cycle". In use, many products have an operational phase and a waiting phase and most reliability failures are caused by degradations occurring during the operational phase. For example, a television set will stay switched off more than it is switched on. By operating it continuously a few months testing will give results from which its reliability over two or three years can be deduced. Of course, the parallel between the accelerated test and real operation will not be exact, but it can be improved by adding switch-off and switch-on cycles and other elaborations. Cars are normally driven for only a few hundred hours each year. By continuous driving, therefore, the equivalent of a year's operation can be achieved in a

[1] IEC Publication 271.

much shorter time. But not all degradation processes will be accelerated by this method, e.g. corrosion processes will be dependent to some extent upon calendar time.

There are methods of accelerated testing other than changing the duty cycle. Many reliability failures are due to the progressive degradation of particular components and these in turn are due to chemical reactions taking place within components, leading, for example, to build-up of impurities. Most chemical reactions go faster if the temperature is raised. For failure mechanisms of this kind the relationship between time to failure and temperature is often given by the equation:

$$\log t_f = A + \frac{B}{T}$$

where t_f is the time to failure, T is the temperature in absolute degrees and A and B are constants. This expression is based on the Arrhenius equation that applies to many chemical reactions. Because the time to failure has a logarithmic relationship with temperature a relatively small increase in temperature can produce a significant reduction in failure time. A rule of thumb that sometimes applies is that a 10°C increase in temperature may halve the time to failure.

Many of the standard environmental tests[1] are, in fact, accelerated life tests, and the list of such tests indicates many of the applied stresses that can be used to investigate a product's reliability. It includes mechanical shock and vibration, low and high temperatures, prolonged periods of storage at high relative humidity and cycles of high and low humidity associated with cycles of temperature change.

PHYSICS OF FAILURE

Another approach to the achievement of reliable products has been given the title of "physics of failure". The idea is that a detailed study of a particular item using the methods of physics and chemistry will reveal possible failure mechanisms and the stresses and stress levels that are likely to activate them. With this knowledge steps can be taken to eliminate the failure mechanisms, thereby improving the reliability of the item. The method is most clearly applicable to components, but this limitation is no real disadvantage, because, as described above, the reliability of a complex product is a composite of the reliability of the components and connections from which it is

[1] IEC Publication 68.

made. Physics of failure studies are, of course, very costly in high-level, research-worker effort, and in practice the reliability of a component is often dominated by simple, workmanship-type defects, which do not need detailed study to characterize, but meticulous control to eliminate.

Accelerated life testing is often used in association with physics of failure studies. Over-stress tests are used to activate failure mechanisms and the detailed study then indicates their quantitative relevance at normal-use conditions. After the component has been improved to eliminate a particular failure mechanism accelerated testing is used to estimate the success of the change.

SYSTEM EFFECTIVENESS

The definition of reliability is quite specific and a range of topics, which do not fall within the definition, have been included in an extended subject called "system effectiveness" in the American technical literature. Early examples of these topics were "availability" and "maintainability". It is argued that the user is not primarily interested in reliability. His concern is with the proportion of time that the product is available for operation related to the cost. This is dependent not only upon the reliability of the product but on other characteristics including its maintainability. A reliability failure will be of less consequence if a repair can be made quickly and cheaply and the product put back into service. Following this path reliability engineering has extended into logistics and cost effectiveness as a technical and mathematical discipline.

MANAGEMENT FOR RELIABILITY

Because of the problem of testing for reliability discussed above necessary reliability characteristics may be difficult to achieve. If some characteristic of the product other than reliability is unsatisfactory, customer reaction is likely to be immediate and insistent, but it may take the customer many months to find that the reliability is inadequate. In the factory, failure to meet most specified performance characteristics will be discovered by test and inspection and will lead to scrap and re-work action. These in turn will give clearly identifiable quality costs and consequent pressure for improvement. But inadequate reliability may well go undiscovered in the factory and no satisfactory method of measuring "reliability costs" has been developed.

For all these reasons reliability may be neglected unless management makes a conscious decision to give it the attention it deserves. The need for this decision becomes ever more insistent because of three characteristics of modern technological industry. First, is the rapid rate of innovation. As discussed above, every new product is a potential reliability hazard, directly proportional to the level of new components and processes it contains. Second, is the pressure for cost reduction. The excessive safety margins of products in the past contributed to their reliability: elimination of too much safety margin in the present can give unreliable products. Third, is the shortness of time allowed for new developments. Reliability may be a problem with a new product rushed into production to meet a particular market opportunity.

In the aerospace and defence industries one management reaction has been to establish separate, strong "reliability assurance" departments. These have taken over from the technical department the design aspects of reliability including component engineering, component failure-rate data information, reliability-prediction activities and redundancy calculations. Similarly, they have taken activities from the quality departments including design review and qualification and reliability testing. Reliability assurance has also been the chosen department for activities in maintainability, availability and system effectiveness.

There is no doubt that, where the magnitude of the activity justifies the establishment of a major department, this is a good way of getting effective work in reliability engineering. For smaller operations it is not practical. Where only a few engineers are justified it is best to recognize that reliability falls between the technical and quality departments and to divide the activity in a pragmatic way between them. The technical department will cover the design, prediction and redundancy activities and the quality department will be made responsible for auditing and reporting, will be involved in reliability testing and will make available its statistical skills.

As a final word: management must decide the level of attention to give to reliability. The system will not make the decision for it. But of all problems in the quality area those of reliability are most serious, because their effects are delayed and their solutions are difficult. Although formal reliability specifications, as part of contracts, are still relatively uncommon, serious work on reliability should not be restricted to projects contractually covered in this way. All products have implicit reliability requirements, and if these are not met customer dissatisfaction is inevitable.

10 Case Studies

The cases illustrate two difficult aspects of modern quality control: the use of zero defects and the qualification testing of new products. Both are based on actual events, but the technical detail has been changed.

START OF A ZERO DEFECTS PROGRAMME

Two Englishmen and an American talked in the dimly lit bar of a large hotel in Madrid. One of the Englishmen spoke emphatically. As always when he felt strongly, his Midland vowels were emphasized.

"Look John, what have you got to lose? You've only got to do it and both you and your manager are bound to get credit. You've already got a better background than the French and look how much glory they got. The company wants these zero-defects programmes. Make any sort of a job of it and everyone will be all over themselves saying how marvellous you are."

The American broke in. He was wearing a large, brightly coloured tie. His vitality crackled from his curling, black hair to his patterned, white and tan brogues. Despite his Southern accent he talked fast.

"I know you, John. You want to do it. You're just building yourself up. You're going straight back to England to give Mike the biggest sales pitch ever. And when you do I'll give you that bottle of Old Grandad."

With a broad grin, hiding his tension John said, "By God Bob, I'll do it. And I'll hold you to that bottle."

Three other members of the European Quality Council, a Swede, a Spaniard and a Belgian, joined the group and the conversation changed to food and flamenco.

A year before, the first Englishman had become company quality manager. The director of operations had asked him what the company should do for Quality and Reliability Year. This was particularly important as the company's principal customer was expressing strong dissatisfaction with product quality. The fact that the customer was expressing the same dissatisfaction with equal truth to its other principal suppliers made it no less unpleasant. His answer had been that the company should start quality-cost reporting using the method devised by the European Quality Council and apply the 14-step quality-improvement programme he had just received in draft from the American director of quality. The proposals were agreed, and he was given a place in the list of presentations for the company's management conference in a month's time. At this all the divisional general managers and their functional department heads—over a hundred managers—would be present.

The draft of the improvement programme was obviously American and it seemed better in the context of a UK Q & R activity to change this. Many months later when the American text had been published in booklet form and translated into seven European languages, it was always recorded that the first translation had been into English.

The English version was printed and issued to the divisions. The presentation was given to the management conference and John, an aggressive, energetic man who had entered the company two years before as the first quality manager of one of its oldest and biggest divisions, started to apply the programme. The division was making a traditional, but very complex, product and had been the subject of particularly strong criticism from the customer.

John went to see his manager, armed with a large flip chart.

"Look Mike, we need this programme. I've got four hundred inspectors and testers screening the stuff and yet the customer's inspections show we're not meeting the AQL on almost all of our products."

He turned over the pages of the flip chart. On each one for a particular product was a graph showing the percentage defective or defects per item found by the customer's inspectors. For two products the graphs straddled the AQL line; for seven others the graphs were way above it—in one case by a factor of eight.

"We're getting some through because we happen to be lucky with the sampling and others at the second or third submission. But any time they really applied the specification they could shut us down. They're pressing for improvement."

Mike had many problems. His production control was a mess and deliveries were late. The prices he got barely gave any profit and certainly not a good return. But he knew John was right. Something had to be done about quality. Even if the actions taken were not very successful it would show willingness and would get the customer off his back for a time.

John broke in again.

"If we really work at it we may save some costs as well as improve the quality."

Mike said "All right John. What do you want to do?"

John was ready with his flip chart.

"I want you to chair a quality-improvement committee with all of the relevant department heads on it—production, purchasing, industrial engineering, engineering, comptroller."

His finger stabbed the organization tree in the chart.

"Ray and his quality engineers have already identified the main defect causes on some of the products."

The flip chart showed Pareto distributions on pieceparts, apparatus and racks.

"What we want is to sort out whose job it is to solve the problems and really get them cracking on them."

Mike looked at his watch.

"Why don't you come back at four o'clock tomorrow and we'll sort out what to do."

The next day the whole pattern had been defined. John would be vice-chairman of the quality-improvement committee. But Mike had insisted that John chair a secondary committee with section heads from the other departments and to which a series of working groups dealing with each product would report.

The programme was introduced at the division staff meeting. The old hands, some of whom had worked on the same product for twenty years, had not taken John seriously before. After all, he had only been there two years. When Mike made the announcement sceptical glances were exchanged, but he quelled the smiles with a hard stare. John hardly noticed, as his words tumbled out and the flip-chart pages turned.

Now a year later there was no question but that the programme had been a success. John's own quality-improvement committee had met regularly every week and reviewed the work of its seven product working parties. Progress on major projects and those falling behind schedule had gone to the main monthly meeting chaired by the division manager. Because of pressure from their own department heads, the members of the working parties from production, engineering and so on had met most of their targets. An industrial engineering study had caused one complex sub-assembly to be divided among six man teams. Specialization and training enabled the difficult adjustments to be made consistently, and for the first time in the industry the AQL, covering over 400 possible defects, was achieved. In a number of shops the defect records of individual operators, as measured by the quality department, were reviewed with them by the production supervisors, so that the operators knew that their own supervisor was really concerned with quality. The design department, which in the past had been too busy with engineering new equipments, had found the time to review a whole series of piecepart tolerances, brought to it by quality engineering. Many had been found to be unnecessarily tight and had been relaxed. Others had been found to be essential and worn machine-shop tools had been replaced. The comptroller had started to measure quality costs on a monthly basis, and their magnitude had been another spur to action.

The consequences had been dramatic. On nine major product lines the percentage defective as measured by the customer had been reduced by a factor of 4. Quality costs in the last quarter of the year were only 5·3 per cent of sales compared with 6·5 per cent in the first quarter. In a period of rising production the inspection and test force had been held constant and in fact some inspectors had transferred to production jobs. The ratio of testers and inspectors to direct operatives had fallen by 21 per cent. Production control was still far from good, but at least it was now hampered to a much smaller degree by continual re-work cycles.

At the meeting in Madrid, John had agreed to widen the scope of quality improvement to involve everyone in the division: managers, engineers, accountants, clerks, salesmen, operators, inspectors. The means of doing this was the zero-defects programme. Once again the support and participation of his division manager was essential, but with his current successes he was much more confident that he would get this than he had been a year ago. The main obstacle was his own fear. Would the old, conservative work force accept the programme or dismiss it as American gimmickry? In his mind's eye he pictured the sober faces of the supervisors' association—their support or lack of it could make or break the programme. Would the cynicism of the middle managers, which had been damped down a year ago, reappear when this new demand was placed upon them? Would the unions refuse to participate or the workers ridicule the programme?

In fact, none of the fears materialized. The only problem with the division manager was that, for his own reasons, he insisted that ZD day be held in four weeks time. The other departments, who had had a year of successful co-operation on the quality-improvement team, gave no sign of cynicism and co-operated enthusiastically in the rush of activity needed to define and prepare the programme for ZD day.

The method by which every member of the division would be involved was worked out and the decision taken not to use the ZD pledge (see Chapter 4). The necessary booklets and pamphlets were written and hurried to printing. The production manager and the quality manager spoke to a meeting of all the supervisors and received a wholehearted promise of support in the important role they would play. A similar meeting with the union representatives, although approached with some misgivings, resulted in an equally positive response. A list of guests was prepared and invitations dispatched.

On the day itself the programme was launched by one of the classical ZD techniques. In the presence of senior representatives of the customer and the company's headquarters the division manager handed letters to each of his department managers.

These pointed out that most people use two quality standards, a personal one, and a lower one they apply at work.

The letter asked questions such as:

At home, would you consider it acceptable, when driving your car, to break down your gatepost or drive accidentally out through the rear wall of your garage, say once or twice a year?

At work, do people think it reasonable to make not more than one or two major errors a year? The division manager then asked that the higher standard be applied at work, "by all of us—in any job at all in the division."

The next stage was for the department managers to repeat the operation with their own section heads.

Before the end of the day every member of the division had been acquainted with the project by his own supervisor and there was complete involvement in ZD from design and development through to shipping.

The division staff and their special guests toured the factory, observing the re-telling of the programme by the various department supervisors. They saw the many posters which had been used to build up interest and the quality-measurement display graphs in each department showing the defect-prevention progress already made. More important, they witnessed the seriousness with which the concept of zero defects was received. Not a single group in the whole plant refused to play its part or gave their supervisor a hard time in his presentation. There was no reason why they should: the quality-improvement efforts and achievements of their management in the past year were proof of the sincerity of the approach.

In a few hours the speeches and the lunch and the photographs of ZD day were over, but John knew, as he received the last congratulations, that the second year of the quality-improvement programme was off to a good start.

During the next week each section's quality-improvement goals would be established. The recognition programme was already worked out and in a few weeks the error-cause removal step (see

Chapter 4) would be launched. By then everyone in the division would have proved to himself that they *could* make a product that "performed exactly like the requirement". That proof would influence the work of the division long after ZD day itself was only a distant memory.

QUALIFICATION TEST OF THE AB 357

Development of the AB 357, a small but complex electromechanical equipment incorporating an electronic control unit, was started by a small team in 1963. Development effort was increased in 1965 and again in 1966. The requirement specification was written and published by the development team in April 1966 and a summary of some of the clauses is given in Table 10.1.

TABLE 10.1

Summary of Some of the Requirements (1966) of the AB 357

Error rate	1×10^{-6} maximum
Time of operation between major overhauls	3,000 hours minimum
Time of operation between maintenance	500 hours minimum
Mean time between failures	1,500 hours minimum
Storage temperature range	−40°C to +70°C
Operating temperature range	−20°C to +50°C
Relative humidity range	20 to 95% throughout the operating temperature range
Allowed supply voltage variation	+10%, −15%
Allowed supply frequency variation	±10 Hz

The equipment consisted of a main functional unit incorporating the electronic control and three sub-units. The principal development innovation was required in the main unit. For the three sub-units designs already in production could be adapted. The difficulty was to achieve the specified high-speed data transmission with an error rate that was sufficiently low. The error rate, which was defined as the proportion of the characters transmitted which were either missing or incorrect, had to be no more than 1 in 1 million. In addition, the reliability of the machine should be very good: otherwise it would not do a satisfactory job for the customer and there would be great difficulty in providing adequate service facilities.

The development was planned to be complete by the beginning of 1968 and production to build up during the second half of the year. However, by mid-1968 all that had been completed were two models of the main unit. Engineering life-tested these and reported quite good results, though they had had to do a certain amount of work during the test to keep the units running, and it was thought that the required error rate and mean time between failures were not really being met, although they had not been measured very carefully.

Meanwhile five prototypes of the main unit were being assembled by Engineering using parts made by Manufacturing, but not on the final production tools, which were not yet available.

A life test of these was started by Engineering in October 1968 and very quickly ran into trouble. Within the first hundred hours of operation two of the machines failed. The failures were both in the new, complex, mechanical assembly, which was subjected to high stresses and accelerations during operation and required machining tolerances during manufacture of extreme precision. The failures were catastrophic, the units destroying themselves. Because they were prepared for the type of failure, the engineers were able to prevent the destruction of the remaining three machines, but the same general pattern of failure was present.

At this stage there was a major upheaval. The technical and marketing staffs at the company level had been following the development and expressing concern that it was late and consequently over budget, but before the events of October 1968 there had been a feeling that the overrun was fairly normal and that the marketing programme, although delayed, had not been seriously prejudiced.

Now there was a complete reversal. Scepticism was expressed at headquarters that the machine ever would be satisfactory. Manufacturing staff at the company level gave great emphasis to the already known fact that the estimated shop cost had risen 60 per cent in the past two years. Marketing expressed doubts about the validity of previously planned export business.

The division itself was at first divided by internal discord. Engineering claimed that the design was basically sound but that the manufactured parts in the models were not to tolerance and this was the reason for breakdown. The quality department, which reported to the manufacturing manager, had done quite a good job in that all parts had been inspected and their deviations from drawing recorded. However the view was expressed that "Quality should have stopped the use of out-of-tolerance parts—that's what they are there for." In the face of the evidence Manufacturing could not dispute that the parts *were* out of tolerance, but did not believe this was the cause of the failure. In any case, without the final tools the tolerances could not be achieved and there was doubt whether they were achievable in regular production anyway.

The fear that the whole project would be stopped caused the division to close its ranks. The manufacturing manager, with the agreement of the company manufacturing staff, went on record that, using the tools and machines on order, the tolerances would be achieved.

The marketing manager claimed that the assured home orders made the product viable, even without export orders. The delay and increased price could be accommodated. The chief development engineer had already introduced design changes, which he was convinced would solve the problem, and came up with a plan for further tests. Ten more main units should be made and life tested: five would be assembled by the engineers and five by Manufacturing. All parts would be inspected by Quality. The tests would be completed by the end of March 1969.

In the face of the division's united and well-argued case for continuance, none of the staff groups at company level were prepared to take the responsibility of recommending ending the project, which would have had very serious business and personal consequences.

The plan for further testing was therefore accepted, but the company had recently become convinced of the need to carry out qualification testing in a formal manner. The company quality director was therefore given the task of ensuring that the test was carried out and reported correctly and objectively.

His discussions with the engineering and quality staff of the division immediately revealed semantic differences in the use of the term "qualification testing". To the division this name was applied only to tests carried out on product made by manufacturing using "hard" tools. These tests were the responsibility of the quality department, but the latter had virtually no involvement in tests, such as those now proposed, carried out on development models. The semantic difficulties were quickly side-stepped when the division's engineers told the company quality director that they knew the units could not possibly meet the specification. To achieve the error rate was out of the question at this stage and it was most unlikely that the specified reliability would be reached either. The purpose of the tests was simply to show that the machines could operate without catastrophic breakdown and that it was worth while to continue with the development. It was agreed the tests would be called prototype tests, but none the less the quality department would audit all the tests and be responsible for reporting the results.

The ten machines were duly assembled by Engineering and Manufacturing and meticulous check was made of all piecepart dimensions. Six parts still presented manufacturing problems and the use of nonconformant parts was agreed by the engineers.

By early March 1969 the ten machines had each completed 1,000 hours (six weeks) of testing and all were still working. However, they had been subjected to routine maintenance every 250 hours, not 500 as specified, and in addition they had broken down and required repair a total of 35 times, giving a mean time between failures of 315 hours. To the suprise of the engineers, only eight of the failures were in the complex mechanical assembly. The rest were in other parts of the unit, which they had thought should have no problems.

Throughout the tests the error rate on each equipment had been monitored many times—643 times in all. Of these measurements 79 per cent had shown an error rate of worse than 1 in 10,000. The engineers' prediction was quite right: the machines did not give the required error rate of 1 in 1 million.

All the results were presented at a large meeting chaired by the managing director. The fact that the machines had survived and that all the manufacturing experts at both division and company level agreed that the key piecepart tolerances could be achieved, carried the day. The engineers also expressed certainty in their ability to achieve the required reliability and error rate. Their confidence was bolstered because over the past few weeks the requirements had been markedly reduced. An error rate of 5×10^{-6} was now accepted as the minimum requirement (1×10^{-6} would remain as a "target") and the mean time between failures had come down to 375 hours. The company quality director emphasized that the 315 hours measured in the test applied to the main unit only: the 375 hours applied to the whole machine—a much more difficult requirement. The 250-hour maintenance period was also accepted. None of these changes was embodied in a specification.

It was agreed that the development would continue throughout 1969 and that an actual qualification test would be performed during the first four months of 1970. A major review was scheduled for early May 1970. Some manufacturing would start before the completion of the tests and sales would start in the second half of 1970. The company quality director emphasized that the qualification test must cover all the sub-units as well as the main unit.

Although the engineers were deeply concerned with improving the main unit, pressed by Quality, they also gave attention to the three existing sub-units. One revealed some operational problems, but they were judged not crucial and re-development was reserved for a later stage. A qualification life test was started on ten each of the other two sub-units. Although these were well-proven variations of the corresponding sub-units of the current product, one immediately gave trouble. It just would not stand up to the higher speed required by the new machine. A work programme was started to develop a replacement. The other sub-unit gave no problem and met its specification.

After a series of requests by the company quality director the requirement specification of the AB 357 was eventually reissued on 12 February 1970, incorporating the agreed changes. The new specification is summarized in Table 10.2.

TABLE 10.2

Summary of Some of the Requirements (Feb. 1970) of the AB 357

Error rate	5×10^{-6} maximum (target 1×10^{-6})
Time of operation between major overhauls	2,000 hours minimum
Time of operation between maintenance	250 hours minimum
Mean time between failures	
whole equipment	375 hours minimum
main unit	750 hours minimum
each sub-unit*	750 hours minimum
Storage temperature range (when packaged)	−40°C to +70°C
Operating temperature range	0°C to +50°C
Relative humidity	Able to withstand $93^{+2}_{-3}\%$ at 40°C for 4 days
Allowed supply voltage variation	+10%, −15%
Allowed supply frequency variation	+0·2Hz, −3 Hz

*Only one sub-unit operates at a time.

Most of the clauses had been made less stringent compared with the optimistic specification of 1966, but Marketing, at both the division and company level, agreed that the changes should not significantly affect the saleability of the product. The situation would, of course, have been quite different if the 1966 specification had been published to the customers. Even though they did not really need the performance indicated they would have, rightly, felt cheated when the product did not live up to its specification.

The units for qualification test were delivered on time and the test started immediately after the New Year festivities. Quality had monitored the manufacture of the machines with its customary care. A significant proportion of the parts were still not in conformance to the drawing, but the critical parts, which had been such a problem a year before, were now correct, and Engineering agreed the other discrepancies were of minor importance.

Within a short time from the start of the test each machine showed a catastrophically high error rate. This was a major shock to the engineers who believed this problem had been completely solved. Investigation showed that it resulted from a change made to the power supply, which was a purchased sub-assembly. Urgent representation to the supplier produced an immediate small design change and a promise that five modified units would be supplied in two weeks and five more one week later.

With the new power supplies fitted, the test re-started and all ten units performed well. The company quality director had been getting reports every two weeks from the divisional quality manager, and ten days before the major review meeting scheduled for 15 May he visited the plant. The test had fallen six weeks behind schedule so that on average only 620 hours of test had been completed on each machine, instead of the required 1,000. However, the situation was already clear. The error-rate specification was being met. The worst machine had an error rate of $4{\cdot}5 \times 10^{-6}$ and the average was $3{\cdot}0 \times 10^{-6}$. This was a dramatic improvement compared with the result obtained a year before and indicated that the single biggest problem had been solved.

One sub-unit had also completed its qualification tests and had passed in all respects. Development of the other sub-unit was not complete. Two of the main units had also passed temperature and humidity tests according to IEC 68 (see Chapter 8) and the limits given in the revised requirement specification.

The problem was the reliability. There had already been 28 failures and the measured mean time between failures was 220 hours. The company quality director pointed out that even if there was not a single additional failure the mtbf at the end of the test would be 360 hours, far worse than the specified requirement of 750 hours. The failure pattern was different from a year previously. Then, some of the failures had indicated problems requiring a major development effort to cure. Now, failure analysis indicated there were thirteen different causes of failure. The company quality director agreed that each one individually was minor: a particular small spring had broken and could easily be strengthened, transistor failures had occurred at a rate higher than predicted, indicating the need to change supplier, and so on.

It would have been ridiculous to abandon the project at this stage. The division's marketing department said that the reliability was really all right. The specified 375 hours mtbf was what they expected after the machine had been in production for many months. This brought a sharp rejoinder from the company quality director. He pointed out that the requirement for the main unit was 750 hours, and that the specification clearly stated that it applied to the qualification test, not to some future field use. It was for this kind of reason that he had been so insistent on getting the requirement specification and qualification test specification defined and re-issued.

The division manager agreed that the requirement was as specified and the units were failing the test. The chief development engineer suggested that all ten test units should be modified to incorporate the corrective actions already indicated and the test be continued for another 1,000 hours. In addition five more units should be made as quickly as possible with the improvements and testing of these started. This plan was finally submitted to the review meeting on 15 May and was accepted.

In the first 200 hours of testing after modification there was a further group of random failures, 10 in all. Then the machines settled down and in the next 800 hours there were only another 7 failures. The mean time between failures for the last 1,000 hours of test was therefore 590 hours, worse than the specification of 750 hours, but for the last 800 hours the mtbf was 1,120 hours.

At this stage it was agreed that, if necessary, a period of "burn-in" would be applied to the units now under manufacture and scheduled for delivery to the first customer in October 1970.

The five additional units started test on 3 July and the first 72 hours was designated as burn-in. Five failures occurred in this period, two on a particular unit. The following 1,000 hours of test gave 6 more failures. The observed mean time between failures was therefore 830 hours, meeting specification. The reduction in sample size from 10 to 5 had, of course, reduced the statistical confidence that the result obtained on the sample under test would be representative of the population of manufactured units. In fact, if the population mtbf was as low as 480 hours there would have been a 10 per cent chance of getting the 6 failures observed or an even smaller number of failures.

Both division and company agreed at the end of August that the qualification test was finally passed and the division quality manager issued a final qualification-test report, summarizing the results obtained. Delivery of the manufactured units to the customer was authorized by the division manager. Because the time between major overhauls was 2,000 hours it was decided to continue the life test on the five units for this period. It was also decided to start life testing one new unit a month and continue for 2,000 hours. This was to give some assurance that the many late engineering changes had been introduced into manufacturing in a controlled and reproducible manner.

The last sub-unit was still a problem. The new design was entirely electronic and "bread-board" models had performed well. If the October delivery date was to be met there was no time for any prolonged testing of production units. Marketing was strongly in favour of taking the risk. Their sales programme was getting under way. To tell customers that deliveries must be put back three months or longer would destroy confidence in the whole project. It might also allow foreign competition to capture a foothold in the market. The quality department argued that much more harm would be done if the first units the customers received did not work properly.

The decision was taken to go ahead on the basis that replacement of the sub-unit on equipment sold in the first six months would take most of the profit, but would not be a disaster. In the end all the sub-units did have to be replaced, because their error rate was unacceptably high. Fortunately, they could be re-worked so the impact on profit was less than it might have been. Marketing claimed that the bad effect this had on the customers was less than would have been caused by delaying delivery, but the quality department was not so sure. The fact that the main unit and the other two sub-units all performed exactly to specification was perhaps the main reason why the deficiencies of the third sub-unit and the inconvenience of replacement were accepted by the customers.

This case is based on the events that took place with a real-life product, although all the numbers are changed. It illustrates the interactions that occur with the different departments involved in launching a new product. It shows that qualification testing and the needed corrective actions revealed by it can cost a large amount of money and seriously delay the completion of a development programme. However, it can help to ensure that the new product does perform satisfactorily as soon as it is introduced into the market and that development effort is kept at a high level until the problems are corrected. There is little doubt in the case considered that, if qualification testing had not been carried out, development effort would have been run down earlier or transferred to cost-reduction activities. Unnecessary performance would have been claimed, which the product would have been incapable of meeting. In addition, almost certainly there would have been a field-reliability problem at a level which might have required replacement of the whole product, not just one sub-unit. All profits would have gone and there would have been a major financial loss: the viability of the project as a whole would have been prejudiced.

Annotated Reading List

1 Crosby, Philip B., *Cutting the Cost of Quality* (Boston, Mass: Industrial Education Institute, 1967)
The original account of a systematic quality-improvement programme by the inventor, now Director–Quality and Vice-President of ITT.

2 Hagan, J. T., *A Management Role for Quality Control* (American Management Association, Inc.)
An important book on quality management by another of ITT's New York quality staff.

3 Halpin, J. F., *Zero Defects* (McGraw-Hill, 1966)
The definitive account of the original zero defects programme in the Martin-Marietta Corporation in 1961–62.

4 Feigenbaum, A. V., *Total Quality Control* (McGraw-Hill, 1961)
Written in 1961, a major advance in the development of quality control as a key management discipline.

5 Duran, J. M., ed., *Handbook of Quality Control* (McGraw-Hill, 2nd edition)
The standard reference book for quality-control techniques.

6 Grant, E. L., *Statistical Quality Control* (McGraw-Hill, 3rd edition 1964)
A good example of the books on statistical quality control written by authors with an academic, mathematical background.

7 Myers, R. H., Wong, K. L., and Gordy, H. M., eds., *Reliability Engineering for Electronic Systems* (Wiley, 1964)
One of the best books on reliability engineering as an advanced technical subject.

8 BS 9001 *Sampling Procedures and Tables for Inspection by Attributes* (British Standards Institution, 1967)

The undisputed leader of sampling plans. Published in the USA as MIL-STD 105D, and in many other countries. Should be in the briefcase of every quality engineer.

9 Defence Guide DG 7A *Sampling Inspection: a Guide to the Use of Defence Specification DEF 131A* (HMSO)
DEF 131A is another name for BS 6001.

10 BS 9000 *Specification for General Requirements for Electronic Parts of Assessed Quality* (British Standards Institution, 1971)
The basic specification of a major series, defining the most advanced system for the quality assurance of purchased electronics components.

11 *Quality Costs What and How* (American Society for Quality Control)
The formal position of the American Society for Quality Control on quality costs.

12 MIL-Q-9858A—*Quality Program Requirements* (US Department of Defense)
The classic specification used by the US Department of Defense to define the quality management system required from its major supplying contractors.

13 MIL-STD-217A—*Reliability Stress and Failure Data for Electronic Equipment* (US Department of Defense)
Probably the most important collection of electronic-component failure-rate data and an account of how to use it in reliability prediction.

14 *Glossary of Terms used in Quality Control* (European Organization for Quality Control, 1969)
The principal glossary for quality control, in fifteen different languages.

15 IEC 271—*Preliminary List of Basic Terms and Definitions for the Reliability of Electronic Equipment and the Components (or Parts) used therein* (International Electrotechnical Commission)
The first of a whole series of important standards on reliability developed and published by one of the major bodies for international standardization.

16 IEC 68—*Basic Environmental Testing Procedures for Electronic Components and Electronic Equipment* (International Electrotechnical Commission)
Another series of important international standards dealing with environmental testing. BS 2001 is the UK equivalent.

17 Nixon, Frank, *Managing to Achieve Quality and Reliability* (McGraw-Hill, 1971). A good book by the founder of modern quality control at Rolls Royce.

Index

ACCELERATED life testing, 157
  effect of temperature, 158
Acceptance inspection, 111
Acceptance number, 89
American Society for Zero Defects, 65
Appraisal quality costs, 17
Approval of suppliers, 117
AQL (acceptable quality level), 162, 195
  definition, 103
  "reasonable", 106
  and sample size, 110
  setting its value, 104
Arrhenius equation, 158
Attribute sampling theory, 88
Audit, 30, 39, 111
  defect-prevention, 61
Availability, 159, 160
Awareness of quality, 58

BINOMIAL, 90
British Post Office, 123
  reliability specification, 151
British Standards Institution, 124
  BS 9000, 124
  BS 9001 (BS 6001), 95
Burghard Committee, 124

CCTU (French) specification, 124
CENEL (European Co-ordinating Committee for Electrical Standards), 129
Certified test record, 125
Chief inspector, 36
  under BS 9000, 128
Component—
  failure rate, 155
  purchasing quality assurance, 124
  specification in development, 135
Comptroller, 20, 30, 32
Conformance, 1, 2, 3
  and cost, 10
  and perfection, 10
  effect on sales, 29
  problem, 34
Consolidated quality report, 77
Consumer's risk, 92
Control limits, 57
Corrective action, 58
  organizational framework, 59
  preventive, 58
  re-work, 58
Cost of ownership, 28
Cost reduction, 76
Crosby, P. B., 44, 47, 65
Cutting the Cost of Quality, 47
CV specifications, 124

DEF 131A, 95
Defect—
  categories, critical, major, minor, 106, 107

Defect (*contd.*)—
  definition, 85
  functional and non-functional, 107
  prevention, 2
  prevention audit, 61
  weighting for quality index, 56
Defective, definition, 85
Defects per week's work, 57
Definition—
  of AQL, 103
  of error, 85
  of failure, 85
  of failure (reliability), 150
  of process average, 103
  of quality, 1
  of quality costs, 3, 11
  of reliability, 148
Department of Defense (USA), 65
Design errors, 147
Design review, 31, 133
  initial, intermediate and final, 134
  pre-meeting report, 134
Development of new products, 16, 130, 149
DG 7A (Defence Guide), 84
Drawing—
  change control, 31
  inspection for errors, 147
Duty cycle, 157

EDUCATION for quality, 81
Electrical Quality Assurance Directorate, 128
Electronic parts of assessed quality, 124
Engineering error control, 146
Environmental testing, 140, 158, 171
Error-cause removal, 70, 71, 165
Error definition, 85
Executive quality council, 45
External failure costs, 19

FAILURE—
  definition, 85
  definition (reliability), 150
  quality costs, 17
  rate, 151, 153

Feigenbaum, A. V., 30
Flow chart for inspection and test, 11
"Fourteen Steps to Quality Improvement", 47
Functional and non-functional defects, 107

GENERAL management—
  and development, 133
  and qualification test, 141, 144
  and quality department, 40
  and quality improvement, 46
  and quality improvement committee, 48
General manager, 7, 40, 46, 48, 73, 76, 82
Generic specifications, 125
Goal setting, 70

HUMAN error, 2
Hypergeometric distribution, 90

IEC (International Electrotechnical Commission), 129
IEC 68 (environmental testing procedures), 140, 158, 171
IEC 271 (reliability terms and definitions), 148, 150, 157
Incoming inspection, 122
Index—
  quality, 56, 76
  quality cost to added shop cost, 25
  quality cost to sales, 24
Inspection—
  and test flow chart, 11
  by attributes, 84
  by sampling, 14, 84, 86
  by variables, 84
  double, multiple and sequential sampling, 84
  level, 101
  level setting, 109
  one hundred per cent, 85
  planning, 32
  reasons for, 85
Inspection, Test, Quality, Manufacturing, 36

Internal failure costs, 19
Isolated lot, 103
ITT—
  quality councils, 44
  quality policy, 6
ITT (Europe), 44

KARLIN, E. W., 61

LIFE testing, 155
  accelerated, 157
Lot—
  acceptance/rejection, 87
  isolated, 103
  size, 99, 101
Lots, series of, 103
LTPD (lot tolerance per cent defective), 95

MAINTAINABILITY, 159, 160
Major defects, 56, 57
Making reliable product, 153
Management action, 111
  for reliability, 159, 160
Management commitment, 48
Managing director, 43, 77
Manpower report, 80
Manufacturing—
  cost variance, 21
  specifications, 3
Matin-Marietta Company, 47, 65, 68
Material review board, 11
Mean time between failures (mtbf), 150, 154
MIL-HDBK 217A (component failure rates), 156
MIL-Q-9858A (quality management), 61
MIL-S-19500C (LTPD sampling), 96
MIL specifications for components, 124
MIL-STD-105D (AQL sampling), 95
MIL-STD-414 (variables sampling), 84
Ministry of Defence, 123
Minor defects, 56, 57

NEW product quality control, 130
Non-functional defects, 107

OBJECTIVES of quality system, 2
One hundred per cent inspection, 85
Operating characteristic (in sampling), 89
Organization of quality department, 35
Over-stress tests, 159

PARETO principle, 50
Percentage defective, "p", chart, 57
Perfection and conformance, 10
Physics of failure, 148
Pledge (zero defects), 68
Poisson distribution, 90
Policies for quality, 6
  top management responsibility, 7
Poster competition, 58
Prediction of reliability, 153
Prevention—
  of defects, 2
  quality costs, 18
Price—
  and delivery, 2
  and quality, 8
Printed board assemblies, 53, 153
Probability of acceptance, 89
Process average, 100
  definition, 103
Producer's risk (in sampling), 92
Product—
  definition, 2
  qualification, 64
  quality auditing, 112
  quality councils, 45
Proving of manufacturing processes, 135
Purchasing, 33
  department (conformance responsibility), 116
  specifications, 115
  specifications (technical responsibility), 116

QUALIFICATION approval, 121, 136
Qualification of new products, 31

Qualification test—
and corrective action, 142
and general management, 144
case study, 166
components and sub-assemblies, 142
conformance to drawings, 139
list of tests, 139
log, 140
"open-ended", 137
organization for, 143
programme managers, 144
purpose, 135
reports, 140, 144
responsibilities of Quality and Technical, 144
specification, 137
supplier/customer relationship, 136
workmanship standards, 139
Qualified products list, 136
Quality—
and general education, 81
audit, 30, 39, 111
awareness, 58, 165
control,
in service industries, 2
of new products, 130, 149
specifications, 4
cost, 8
comptroller responsibility for reporting, 20
conventional categorization, 18
definition and categorization, 3, 11
design changes, 17
identifying defective items, 11
improving inspection effectiveness, 16
indices, 24
internal and external failure, 19
management motivation, 24
overheads, 21
preventing defective items, 16
prevention, appraisal, failure, 18
purposes of reporting, 23
reduction, 27, 76
replacing defective items, 11
reporting, 20, 23, 51
sub-categories, 19
target setting for reduction, 26
warranty, 13
wider aspects, 27
councils, 44, 72
executive, 45
product, 45
regional, 44
world-wide, 45
definition, 1
department,
and general manager, 73
isolation, 41
need for independence, 40
organization and functions, 30, 40
director, 77
engineers in development, 132
improvement,
goals, 165
programme, 46
team, 50
team chairman, 50
team responsibilities, 50
through defect prevention, 47
index, 56, 76
management, 30, 41
manpower report, 80
manual of supplier, 119, 120
measurement, 51, 165
examples of methods, 52
objectives of business, 2
policies, 6, 48
price and cost, 8
problem solving, 33
program specification, 61
reliability year, 148, 162
reports, 74
consolidated, 77
responsibilities,
of comptroller's department, 31
of design/development department, 31
of marketing department, 31
of manufacturing department, 31
of purchasing department, 31, 116

Quality (*contd.*)—
system elements, 62

RECOGNITION, 70, 72, 165
Recruiting of quality staff, 81
Reduced inspection, 113
Redundancy, 156
active and passive, 157
Regional quality councils, 44
Release of product for manufacturing, 136
Reliability, 148
and simplicity, 154
assurance, department, 160
definition, 148
differentiation from quality, 149
in contracts, 160
prediction, 153
prediction difficulties, 155
problem, 149
specialists, 148
Re-qualification, 64
Responsibility for outgoing quality, 111
Risk (producer's and customer's), 92

SAMPLE size and AQL, 110
Sampling inspection, 14, 84, 86
Savings in quality cost, 27
Screening out defectives, 11, 85, 87
Semiconductor integrated circuit, 153
Series of lots, 103
Service industries, 11
Setting the AQL, 104
Setting the inspection level, 109
Solder joint, 108, 153
Soldering, 53
Source control, 123, 128
Source inspection, 123
Span of control, 36
Specifications—
general, generic, detail, 125
manufacturing, 3
purchasing, 115
qualification test, 137
quality control, 4
six different types, 6
test and inspection in development, 135
Staff quality directors, 41, 42
Staff turnover rate reduction, 66
Standard cost, 21
Statistical quality control, 57, 73
Sub-contracting, 33
Supplier—
approval, 117
continuing quality assurance, 122
quality control, 115
survey, 117
check list, 118
quality manual, 119
references, 119
System effectiveness, 159, 160

TARGET setting for quality cost reduction, 26
Telephone exchange reliability, 151
Test planning, 32
Testing—
and inspection, 135
by producer or consumer, 96
environmental, 140, 158, 171
Theory of attribute sampling, 88
Tightened inspection, 100, 103, 113
Top management responsibility for quality policy, 7
Total quality control, 30
Trade unions, 68
Training for quality, 33, 81
Transistor reliability, 151

WARRANTY costs, 13, 21
Weighting of defects, 56
Work-in-process inventory, 61
Workmanship—
defects and reliability, 159
standards and qualification testing, 139
Work study, 16
World-wide quality council, 45

ZD day, 67
ZD pledge, 68
Zero defects, 65, 161